PORTUGAL'S
POUSADA ROUTE

Stuart Ross

VISTA IBÉRICA PUBLICAÇÕES

First published, 1986.
Second edition wholly revised, 1992.
Portuguese and German translations, 1992
Reprinted, 1993
Third edition (Second German & Portruguese), 1994

Published by Vista Ibérica Publicações,
Len Port (Editor), Peter Daughtrey (Designer),
No. Contribuinte 900398086
Largo 5 de Outubro, 8400 Lagoa.,
Algarve, Portugal.

Printed by Sociedade Tipográfica S.A. Sacavém.

ISBN: 972-8044-00-3
Depósito Legal No. 77697/94

It is the intention of the author and publishers to bring out a revised edition of this book annually. All suggestions from readers about up-dating the information will be most gratefully received at Largo 5 de Outubro, 8400 Lagoa, Algarve, Portugal. Tel/fax: 351 082 52370

Front cover: *The castle pousada at Alvito.* LP
Inside cover: *The hilltop fortress at Marvão.* E

PHOTOGRAPHS

The British-born photojournalist MARION KAPLAN took most of the phoptographs in this book. After spending more than 20 years as a freelance photographer in Africa contributing to some of the world's most distinguished magazines and newspapers, she turned her focus to Europe. From the Algarve, she travelled throughout Portrugal capturing remarkable images of the land and its people for a number of publications, including *National Geographic, Reader's Digest* and the *New York Times*. She is the author of two books, *Focus Africa* and more recently *The Portuguese: The Land and its People*, published by Viking Penguin. Other photographs are by Stuart Ross and Len Port or are reproduced with the kind permission of Enatur.

CONTENTS

Preface   page   8
Introduction   10
Pousadas and their locations
1   São Teotónio, Valença   14
2   Dom Denis,
    Vila Nova de Cerveira   18
3   São Bento, Caniçada   22
4   Nossa Senhora de Oliveira,
    Guimarães   28
5   Santa Marinha da Costa,
    Guimarães   32
6   São Bartolomeu, Bragança   38
7   Santa Catarina,
    Miranda do Douro   42
8   Barão Forrester, Alijó   46
9   São Gonçalo, Amarante   50
10 Santa das Neves, Almeida   54
11 da Ria, Aveiro   58
12 Santo António, Serém   62
13 São Jerónimo, Caramulo   66
14 Santa Barbara, Oliveira do
    Hospital   70
15 S. Lourenço, Manteigas   74
16 Mestre A. Domingues,
    Batalha   78
17 do Castelo, Óbidos   82
18 de Palmela, Palmela   88
19 São Filipe, Setúbal   94
20 São Pedro, Castelo do
    Bode   100

CONTENTS

21 Stª Maria, Marvão 104
22 Rainha Santa Isabel,
   Estremoz 108
23 Santa Luzia, Elvas 114
24 Dos Lóios, Évora 118
25 Vale do Gaio,
   Alcaçer do Sal 124
26 São Tiago
   Santiago de Caçem 128
27 São Gens, Serpa 132
28 Santa Clara,
   Santa Clara-a-Velha 136
29 São Brás, Sãο΄Brás
   de Alportel 140
30 do Infante, Sagres 144
31 Quinta da Ortiga,
   Santo do Cacém 148
32 Santa Cristina,
   Condeixa-a-Nova 150
33 São Miguel, Sousel 154
34 de Monsanto,
   Monsanto 158

35 Castelo, Alvito 164

Update 170

Getting underway 173

Distance / temperature 176

General information 181

Town index 184

PREFACE

In order to prepare this third edition I revisited all of Portugal's pousadas. In doing so I was struck by the enormous improvements that have taken place since 1986 when the first edition was published. The improvements have been not only in the pousadas themselves, but in the road network throughout the country. This made my task simpler and even more enjoyable. Standards of service and food are much higher; so are prices - but the increases are no greater than in other European countries and prices still represent very good value for money.

After nearly 30 years of staying in pousadas I have become increasingly aware that, apart from publicity-orientated leaflets from tourist offices, there is no single publication giving details of where they are all located, advice on how to reserve accommodation, how to get there, what facilities they have and what to see in surrounding areas.

I felt an unbiased opinion of what was good, both with the pousada and the area in which it was located, would be of help to intending visitors. In travelling around a country, particularly in a limited holiday period, one cannot afford to make too many mistakes. I have included tables showing roughly the distance and the average driving time between each pousada. Hopefully they will be helpful in planning your itinerary. I hope too that this guidebook will help you to avoid the difficulties, disappointments and frustrations I have sometimes experienced.

Wherever possible I have consulted other guests in an endeavour to reach a fair conclusion. Individual opinions varied from the over-enthusiastic to the destructively cynical. I have tried to adopt an independent middle course and to provide information concerning each pousada which may add to the pleasure of your stay.

In times of rapidly changing political, social and economic conditions, it would be surprising if the opinions expressed here were not similarly subject to revision in some cases. The management and staff of pousadas change. Standards change. Telephone numbers are for ever changing. Every care has been taken to avoid inaccuracies and errors, but it is difficult to ensure that none occurs.

The fact that I have enjoyed writing this third edition even more than the first two is due, as I have said, to improved standards and also to the support I have received from many people who made time to see me, answer my questions, and point me in the direction of interesting avenues of enquiry. I am particularly grateful to ENATUR (Empresa Nacional de Turismo - the Government agency which runs the pousadas) and to those who accompanied me throughout the tour.

Finally, thank you Portugal for being such a lovely and hospitable country.

STUART ROSS

Serra de Monchique.

Opposite: *The floodlit facade of Santa Marinha pousada.* SR

INTRODUCTION

The word pousada comes from the Portuguese verb 'pousar', which the dictionary translates as 'to lay down a burden, to lodge at, to repose'. The pousadas form a network of Government-owned hostelries ranging from the relatively simple to the opulent. They are situated throughout Portugal and ensure a high standard of comfort.

To visit them is to take advantage of the scenery surrounding their priviledged locations, often removed from populated areas and the better-known tourist itineraries. They also provide an opportunity of acquiring a knowledge of the culture, customs and cuisine of the various regions in this lovely country.

The references to road numbers and distances relate to Michelin map 37 of Portugal, or Mapa do Estado das Estradas issued by Automóvel Clube de Portugal whose head office is 24-26, Rua Rosa Araújo, 1114 Lisbon. Another useful map is the Turinta road map produced in Portugal, which also indicates places of historical interest and includes a guide to restaurants, bars and other establishments.

Distances and driving times between pousadas have been included in this book. The pousadas have been graded by ENATUR who operate them. In order to avoid confusion we have adopted the same four grades:

CH (Chateaux) is the top grade, equating to five-star hotels, and usually located in buildings of historical interest like castles, monasteries and convents.

B, C and C Superior are the equivelent of 3 and 4-star hotels and are often purpose-built, or conversions of residences either used formerly for specific government purposes or as private homes.

There are three tariffs depending on the season:

Low - 1st November to 31st March (except Christmas, New Year and Easter when high season rates apply).

Middle - 1st April to 30th June and from 1st to 31st October.

High - 1st July to 30th September.

The rates at the time of going to press were as set out in the table below.

Included with the details of each pousada are the telephone, fax and telex numbers and the grading. The central reservation telephone, fax and telex numbers are on page 170. In practice you may find, if your itinerary has not already been arranged before departure, that the pousada where you are staying can be very

1995	MIDDLE SEASON 1/4 to 30/6 and 1/10 to 31/10				HIGH SEASON 1/7 to 30/9				LOW SEASON 1/11/94 to 31/3/95			
GRADE	"B"	"C"	"CS"	"CH"	"B"	"C"	"CS"	"CH"	"B"	"C"	"CS"	"CH"
DOUBLE	12.000$	16.000$	17.500$	22.000$	13.500$	19.000$	21.500$	27.000$	8.800$	10.800$	13.900$	16.900$
SINGLE	10.000$	14.000$	15.500$	19.000$	11.500$	17.000$	18.500$	24.000$	7.300$	9.000$	12.100$	14.400$
SUITE	16.500$	21.000$	23.500$	29.000$	19.500$	25.000$	28.000$	35.500$	11.400$	14.000$	17.800$	20.000$
				40.000$				48.500$				35.000$
EXTRA BED	3.500$	5.000$	5.500$	7.000$	4.000$	6.000$	6.500$	8.000$	2.700$	3.300$	4.300$	5.200$
Note: 30/12 to 1/1 and 24/2 to 28/2 middle season rates apply.												

helpful in telexing or telephoning ahead to make subsequent reservations.

It is as well to remember that the number of tourists visiting Portugal approaches 10 million each year and that the demand for accommodation often exceeds supply, particularly during the high season when early planning and booking is essential if you are not to be disappointed in obtaining a bedroom in the pousada of your choice.

There is considerable autonomy in each of the pousadas. This greatly adds to their individuality and character and avoids a faceless, soulless state-run atmosphere. Because of this autonomy there is a variation in times of meals and booking in. It is essential to check the latest time up to which reserved accommodation will be held. Portugal operates a 24-hour clock. Unless payment has been made in advance, you must arrive by the stipulated time. This usually varies between 1800 and 2000 hrs (6 pm to 8 pm) but it can be earlier. The same applies to booking out. It varies between 0800 and 1000 hrs (8 am to 10 am) and rooms should be vacated by noon.

Restaurant times are, again, the decision of the individual management. As a guide, meals are available as follows: Breakfast 0730 - 1000 (7.30am - 10 am) available in your bedroom without extra charge. Lunch 1230 - 1500 (12.30 pm - 3 pm). Dinner 1930 - 2100 (7.30 pm - 9 pm) and sometimes later.

The Portuguese, of course, find our 12-hour clock as confusing as some visitors find the 24-hour method. Don't be surprised, therefore, to discover you may have dinner 'until 2200 am'. Anyway, on holiday, a glass of port at 2200 am is as good a time as any !

Despite the risk of occasional rain, there is much to be said for low and middle season travel as the centre of Portugal can be uncomfortably hot in the height of summer with temperatures of 37 degrees Centigrade (98 Fahrenheit) quite common. An air-conditioned car in midsummer is a luxury and an extravagance you will not regret.

There is no limit to the length of stay but in practice, owing to demand in the high season, you are unlikely to obtain accommodation for more than one or two nights in any one pousada.

Dogs are generally not admitted. It is, however, at the discretion of the management and we have found at the smaller pousadas, out of season, the attitude is fairly relaxed.

Even if there is no official laundry service and you are staying for more than a night, there is always someone who, without the aid of the latest washing-machine, manages to return shirts, blouses and underwear in immaculate condition.

All pousadas accept credit cards. A service charge is included, but a tip for friendly and helpful assistance is always appreciated. It is surprising how often it is more than warranted.

The last pousada to be completed was at Sousel in Alentejo (see page 154). There are plans to convert the convents and monastaries at Tomar, Crato, Beja and Braga. Further pousadas are planned for Berlenga Island, Arganil and Queluz. Future editions of this guide will include details of new pousadas as information about them is officially released.

In the past, some of the pousadas have

been difficult to find, especially for a foreigner with little or no knowledge of Portuguese. Recognising this, ENATUR have installed 900 new signs - like the one illustrated opposite - in reflecting lettering on a blue background, showing the distance in kilometres.

Also illustrated on this page are the symbols used throughout the book to show the location, facilities and recreational activities at each pousada.

FACILITIES

	Air Conditioning
	Telex
	Money Exchange
	Satellite TV
	Credit Cards
	Convention Halls

RECREATION

	Swimming Pool
	Tennis Court
	Fishing
	Nautic Sports
	Golf
	Hunting
	Esplanade

LOCATION

	In National Monument		Regional Pousada
	In Historical Zone		

SÃO TEOTÓNIO • VALENÇA

THE AREA

The river Minho, which the pousada overlooks, forms Portugal's northern boundary with Spain. The area has seen some turbulent times and the number of forts along the frontier are a reminder of less peaceful days. Now it is a popular holiday area in the summer with two spas (Melgaço and Monção) nearby. The roads 101 and 202 follow the river to the east and after passing through these spa towns, reach the frontier at S. Gregório (50 kms). You may arrive in Valença via the bridge from Tuy in Spain. This bridge was built by the ubiquitous Eiffel in 1885. There is a good view of it from the pousada. There are also several river crossings by ferry, one at Monção and one at Vila Nova de Cerveira. A new bridge opened in 1993.

A good circular trip is to follow the Minho to its mouth (Foz de Minho) on the RN 13 (now designated E 50), and then south along the Atlantic coast to Viana do Castelo where a stop to have a look at the town centre makes sense. Enatur run a large, elegant hotel here called Hotel Sta Luzia. The Praça da República, with its fountain and palace, is particularly attractive. By accommodating the town hall (câmara) in the Távoras Palace, the local councillors have done themselves proud. After Viana do Castelo, turn inland, following the north bank of the river Lima (RN 202) to Ponte de Lima, where you have the alternative of returning to base via the 201 or continuing, this time on the south bank (RN 203), to Ponte da Barca. After a look at this quaint riverside town, turn north (RN 101) for the homeward run via Arcos de Valdevez and Monção. This is the area of country houses and of distinctive granaries (*espigueiros*) built on stone stilts to preserve the corn from predators. The granaries are often decorated with a stone cross and can be mistaken for important tombs of former landowners. Of all the country houses seen en route there is nothing to rival the Brejoeira Palace. Travelling north, it is on the lefthand side of the road about 5 kms south of Monção. Although access even to the grounds is not permitted, it is nice to stand and stare. Built in the first half of the 19th century on much the same lines as the Ajuda Palace in Lisbon, it was sold at public auction in 1901. While entry to Brejoeira is beyond one's hopes, there are other palaces in the area which take in paying guests. Palace da Glória at Jolda (Arcos de Valdevez), Palace Vedro at Vedro de Magalhães (Ponte de Barca) and Palace de Calheiros at Ponte de Lima are three. Further details can be obtained from the Associação do Turismo de Habitação (TURIHAB), Praça da República, 4990 Ponte de Lima. One snag for some travellers - the minimum stay is three nights.

The other sight on the journey is the vines growing on their supports which give the grapes for the vinho verde wines. This area is the heart of vinho verde wine making. There is a tourist office in the new part of Valença which has some literature on the region in several languages.

Top left: *Stilted corn stores.* MK
Centre & bottom right: *August festival of Senhora d'Agonia.* MK
Bottom left: *Eiffel's bridge over the Minho river.* SR

15

SÃO TEOTÓNIO • VALENÇA

THE POUSADA São Teotónio is one category lower than its neighbour, Dom Dinis at Vila Nova de Cerveira. Named after Portugal's first saint, it was purpose-built in 1962 and in some ways is more practical than its plushier rival, particularly in layout. It is well-established and popular, with lovely river views from the reception rooms and spacious bedrooms. It is not a bad thing from the visitor's viewpoint to have two pousadas so close. It ensures a healthy rivalry and high standards. São Teotónio has a commanding position at the north-east corner of the battlements within the fortress overlooking Tuy, the Spanish equivalent, on the other side of the frontier bridge.

Valença is a great tourist attraction and despite the inevitable souvenir shops geared to this passing trade, the town has retained its charm with its narrow cobbled streets, squares and fountains. It is reminiscent of Óbidos, north of Lisbon, where there is another pousada. Fortunately, both towns are scheduled as national monuments.

The origin of the town is uncertain,

but from Roman times it was known as Contrasta. At the beginning of the 13th century King Sancho I erected a castle here. King Afonso III (1245 - 1279) changed the name to Valença; quite why is not clear. Several succeeding kings continued defensive works and by the beginning of the 18th century the town had become one of the most important and largest fortresses in Portugal. It resembles a French fort in the de Vauban style - a double fortress connected by a bridge spanning a wide and deep ditch. The emblazoned gateways were guarded by cannons which are still in place around the ramparts. Traffic lights, not cannons now control the gateways. Despite several sieges, some by the French, the original fortifications are in a very good state of preservation and are best explored on foot which can be done very easily from the pousada. There are a couple of chapels, São Sebastião and Bom Jesus, complemented by two powder magazines, in the Coroada part of the outer fort. 'Coroada' is a corruption of *'obra coroa'* so named because of the similarity in the plan of

HOW TO FIND
Easy. Inside the old fortress in Valença, on the north-east corner overlooking the bridge across the river into Spain. Valença is in the far north of Portugal on the road on the Portuguese side of the River Minho.

Tel: **(051) 82 242/52**
Fax: **(051) 824397** Telex: **32827**

FACILITIES

GRADE
C^Sup

The pousada. E

this part to a royal crown.

Back at the pousada after your wanderings, the food should please you. There is an à la carte menu of 24 dishes in addition to the set menu. The area is noted for smoked hams and caldo verde (a seasoned vegetable soup). The pousada does both well. Trutas do Rio Coura Recheadas (the Minho's special way of grilling trout with a flavouring of smoked bacon, which is inserted before cooking) is a mouth-watering delight. Also try Rojões de Porco (cubes of roasted pork meat) or Cabrito à Serrana and Vitela Assada à Costa Verde (goat and veal

respectively). Salmon and lampreys from the river Minho are often on the menu, and the chef also produces a good Arroz de Marisco à Poveira (rice and shellfish). There is a large selection of vinho verdes and wines from other regions. Although we have not sampled them yet, there is a recommended red and white from Monção.

Looking across the Minho as the lights come on in Spain, you are conscious of the closeness of another country with its own separate culture and customs. On whichever side of the border you come to rest for the night, it would be difficult to beat the Pousada de São Teotónio.

DOM DINIS • VILA NOVA DE CERVEIRA

THE AREA
Much of the chapter on the neighbouring pousada at Valença applies equally to the fortress of Dom Dinis which was built in the late 13th or early 14th centuries.ignored, or given only passing reference in the guide books, the *Tesouros Artísticos de Portugal* gives the date of construction as during the reign of King Afonso III, but an official report by the Secretary of State for Public Works and the Director General of National Buildings and Monuments is explicit in stating that King Dinis ordered the construction and gave the charter on 1st October 1321. This is not as big a discrepancy as it may seem. Afonso, who died in 1279, was succeeded by Dom Dinis. It is possible that plans were discussed towards the end of Afonso's reign, leaving his successor to implement the building of the fortress.

The design of the town was oval in shape with houses and churches within the fortress walls. Substantial changes and improvements took place in the 15th and 16th centuries and, on the 25th September 1643, the garrison successfully withstood a determined attack by the Spanish. Spain and Portugal then entered a period of peace and these frontier fortifications lost their strategic importance and fell into disuse. Outside the fortress walls the town is pleasant and expanding, with the 18th-century Igreja Matriz (parish church) not far from the pousada's entrance. The memorial dated 1809 opposite the pousada entrance and the church is to honour those Portuguese who gave their lives successfully repelling a Napoleonic attack led by General Soult in Cerveira that year.

Vila Nova de Cerveira is roughly halfway between Viana do Castelo on the Atlantic coast and Monção further up the river Minho. Both are interesting, and Valença and Melgaço (where there is a spa) also deserve a visit. Monção is an old fortified town which has played much the same role in Portugal's history as many other of these frontier outposts. The town centres itself around two main squares - Praça da República and Praça Deu-la-Deu. The latter is named after Senhora Deuladeu Martins who, in 1368 when the town had been surrounded by the troops of Henry II of Castile, had the bright idea of cooking some bread and throwing it to the enemy. Obviously, thought the invading commander, a garrison that has surplus food must be so well victualled that there is no hope of surrender. He withdrew! The parish church and its chapel of S. Sebastião date from the early 12th century when Portugal first became an independent country.

East of Vila Nova de Cerveira on the RN 101 and 202 and some 8 kms this side of Melgaço, a Roman bridge spans the river Mouro. History was made here. A meeting took place on Thursday 1st November 1386 between John of Gaunt (Edward III's son) and João I. The result of this meeting was the marriage the following year between John of Gaunt's daughter (Philippa of Lancaster) and King João. This was the start of the longest alliance in history.

Fishing on the Minho is a popular pastime. Trout, perch, grayling, bass and barbel are about if you are lucky. The tourist offices will give you details and often put you in touch with local anglers.

Opposite: *High Minho haystacks.* MK

DOM DINIS • VILA NOVA DE CERVEIRA

THE POUSADA

The idea of converting this disused fortress into a pousada goes back to 1971, but it was not until 1982 that the object was achieved and Dom Dinis was opened. The 29 spacious, air-conditioned bedrooms are in three separate blocks - block A with seven, and B and C each with eleven bedrooms. The bar, disco and a sitting-room are in a separate building, reputedly at one time used as the garrison prison. The dining-room, banquet/breakfast-room are in another separate building. The dining-room is perched like a huge greenhouse on top of this walled town with fabulous views across the Minho to Spain.

The architect's intention of maintaining the personality of a garrison is clear. Architecturally there is much to be said for preserving the original buildings individually. Nevertheless, it is not one of the most successful castle conversions when compared with Óbidos, Estremoz or Palmela.

The layout is very pleasant on a balmy summer's evening, but its impracticality is highlighted in wet, windy or cold weather. In good weather it is romantic to stroll from your bedroom to the prison bar and, after drinks, to meander across to the dining-room. It is quite another matter on a wet and windy night. You arrive for the soup looking as though you have just survived a long stretch 'inside' for 'absence without leave' ! However, the management supplies ample umbrellas to get you from one section to another, and certainly the staff cannot do enough to ensure guests' comfort.

When the first edition of this guide was published the food was no more than adequate for a pousada then rated as one of the top seven in the country. Things have much improved. In addition to the set menu which changes daily, there is an extensive à la carte choice. Although the meat and poultry dishes are now very good, the pousada has gained a fine reputation for local fish which include river salmon, trout and lampreys. Vinho verde wine must be sampled before leaving the Minho. The Alvarinhos, on their home ground, are reckoned to be the best. There is a good list, and wines from Ponta da Barca and Ponte de Lima are recommended.

HOW TO FIND

Easy. Inside the old fortifications in the town of Vila Nova de Cerveira. Like Valença (13 kms south -west), Vila Nova de Cerveira stands on the River Minho, 39 kms from Viana do Castelo (on the coast).

Tel: **(051) 795601**

Fax: **(051) 795604** Telex: **32821**

FACILITIES

GRADE

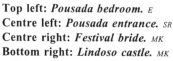

Top left: *Pousada bedroom.* E
Centre left: *Pousada entrance.* SR
Centre right: *Festival bride.* MK
Bottom right: *Lindoso castle.* MK

Two little chapels, one over the entrance and one in the perimter wall deserve a visit - if you can get in. Secular and ecclesiastical authorities do not combine to make access easy. The pillory in the grounds dates from 1547.

At night, the gentle floodlighting of the fortress accentuates the charm of old stone. The church clock, which repeats its strike on the hour, adds to the atmosphere. One sleeps safely within the ramparts.

SÃO BENTO • BARRAGEM DA CANIÇADA

THE AREA

We are now among the best scenery that Portugal, if not Europe, has to offer. Standing on the upper slopes of the Serra do Gerês or on the Serra do Barroso, the river Cavado way, way below, looks minute. Even the great lakes along its course look like puddles, and the houses around the shore appear merely as specks. There are a million and one places from which to enjoy the scenery, but probably none better than from the terrace of the pousada.

Gerês, the nearest town, is a popular spa. King Luis I took the cure there in 1888. It was not as efficacious as he hoped - he died the following year. In the pump room and some of the rather faded hotels there is a hint.of its former glory. The whole area forms part of the National Park of Peneda-Gerês, an area of about 70,000 hectares (175,000 square miles). This is a nature reserve where bird-watchers have every chance of seeing a wide range of species including eagles. Also in the park are wild ponies and pigs, deer, wolves and genets whose chances of survival are much greater than outside the perimeter. The National Park has a good information office just south of Gerês and the tourist office in the crescent by the pump room can give the answers to most questions. There are suggested walks to suit the individual. For a debut try Pedra Bela (6.5 kms) or if you want a sterner test try Bouça da Mó (20 kms). The tourist office will tell you the nearest point a taxi can reach. Walking always seems easier when there is a lift back.

Exploring this national park, like the park more recently designated north of Bragança, is rewarding for the lover of flora and fauna. It is equally rewarding for those who just like strolling amid the scents and sounds of streams and forest. If you want to shoot or fish, details can be obtained at the pousada or from the tourist offices. In the main, the park is concerned with conservation so that these sports are very strictly controlled and restricted.

The N 101 from the north meets the N 308 which skirts the *barragem* (dam) at the foot of the mountains and proceeds through some truly delightful countryside. There are so many different trees, it is difficult to recognise them all. An identification book is again useful. The commoner trees include plane, chestnut, eucalyptus, fir, birch, and oak. There is plenty of heather sweeping up towards the dusting of winter snow on the peaks which rise to 1500 metres.

Braga is about 50 kms, and Oporto 100 kms, but these are better explored at another time. Use your stay here as a breathing space - a place to unwind if saturation point has been reached with architectural and historical splendours.

Opposite top: *Yolked oxen at work.* MK
Opposite bottom: *Harvesting vinho verde grapes.* MK
Page 25: *The pousada.* SR

SÃO BENTO • BARRAGEM DA CANIÇADA

THE POUSADA
An 'away from it all' feeling greets you on driving into the courtyard. This lovely hostelry is aesthetically one of the most successful of the modern pousadas. Unlike many pousadas overlooking *barragems*, it is not an adaptation of buildings used in the dam's construction (1952 - 1954). Originally a small private hotel, it was aquired as a pousada in 1968 and has an established reputation for food and comfort. The central heating and galleried *sala* (sitting room) make for a cosy sojurn even in winter. The high ceilings are in wood, supported on joists with massive rafters and purlins, all adding to the hunting lodge atmosphere. The large shaded picture windows overlooking the lake and mountains make it pleasantly cool in summer.

Exercise, however gentle, is necessary if justice is to be done to the chef's daily specialities or the à la carte menu, which includes regional dishes of the Minho. Thoughtfully, a swimming pool and a tennis court have been built in the grounds and the use of these amenities should give just the appetite needed.

Some of the dishes on the à la carte menu take 20 - 30 minutes to prepare. They are worth the wait. We would recommend Arroz de Pato à moda de Braga (duck risotto) and many of the game dishes are also very good indeed. Although we haven't tried it here, Rojões, a pork dish typical of the Minho, is unusual and has its devotees.

Before your meal, have a chat with the head waiter. He wants you to enjoy the country's cuisine just as much as you do. The two Manuels who wait at table have over 40 years service between them.

There are three dozen different wines, 13 in half bottles. Unless by medical or financial decree, this is not a place for half bottles or pinchpenny dining. Treat yourself to the best of the vinho verdes like Alvarinho Palácio da Brejoeiro which is ridiculously expensive, but one look at the palace near Monção and you realise why. One of the last great country mansions to be built (1834) and modelled on the Ajuda Palace in Lisbon, it is most impressive.

If you want to try red vinho verdes, Ponte de Lima and Ponte da Barca are included. To see where they come from,

HOW TO FIND

Needs care. Take the main road running east from Braga to Chaves. After about 30kms, there is a road on the left to Caniçada village and Caldas do Gerês. After about 1 km, the pousada is on your right.

Tel: **(053) 647190/1**
Fax: **(053) 647867** Telex: **32339**

FACILITIES

RECREATION

GRADE

SÃO BENTO • BARRAGEM DA CANIÇADA

follow the river Lima inland from Viana do Castelo. To know the origin of a wine always adds to its interest. For those who find the Vinho verdes too acid, the Sogrape reds are reliable. Frei João is a good Bairrada, but the older Reservas can be expensive. The Alianças in red or white are cheaper and good value.

On the subject of wines, if you are travelling east to Trás-os-Montes on the N 103, before entering Chaves a turning on the right (N 312) leads to Boticas the home of the sinister-sounding Vinho dos Mortos (wine of the dead). Dona Luisa Leite, at the pousada Santa Catarina, Miranda do Douro, herself a native of Chaves, told us that wine was buried to avoid confiscation during the Napoleonic wars. When exhumed it was discovered that the colour and taste had improved. It is still matured

in this way, but is difficult to come by.

Caniçada has proved so popular that additional bedrooms were added in 1990. The architect, Eduardo Coimbra Brito, is to be congratulated for incorporating the additional 12 bedrooms without in any way detracting from the vernacular charm of the original.

Named after the nearby village of São Bento de Porta Aberta, the open doors of this pousada will offer you a generous welcome and ensure your stay is a memorable one.

Top: *Folk dancing.* MK
Opposite: *Peneda-Gerês National Park.* E

N. SRA. DE OLIVEIRA • GUIMARÃES

THE AREA
Guimarães was the original capital of Portugal and birthplace of Afonso Henriques (1139-85), the country's first king. It is a lovely old town steeped in history and rightly called the cradle of Portugal. Its plethora of churches, chapels, convents and museums make it happy fodder for the guidebooks but the stamp of Guimarães is indelibly printed in the memory in the minor houses, emblazoned with coats of arms, in the arcaded streets with pillars rubbed smooth by centuries of passers-by, and in the narrow alley-ways with verandahs leaning forward to greet their opposite neighbours.

At the foot of the 10th-century castle where Afonso Henriques was born, is the massive Ducal Palace erected by the first Duke of Bragança in the 15th century. The Braganças ruled Portugal from 1640 until the fall of the monarchy in 1910. Most visitors find the interior furniture and furnishings more agreeable than the rather forbidding and uncompromising lines of the exterior.

In the Largo da Oliveira, the pousada is ideally situated for exploring the many attractions of the town's centre. A street map is useful and one can be obtained from the tourist office in the corner of the Alameda da Liberdade gardens, south of the pousada. Close by, the São Francisco and the Santos Passos churches in Largos da República and do Brazil can be inspected. In the Rua Santa Maria, which runs from the pousada's square, the local councillors have installed themselves in what was the Convento de Santa Clara, a fine building with a baroque façade built in 1741. At the rear, have a glimpse at the

Praça de Santiago. In the Largo da Oliveira itself is the crenellated Paços do Concelho commenced during King João's reign (1385-1433). At street level are massive arches giving welcome shade after crossing the square in the hot summer, and on the first floor is a public library by courtesy of the Gulbenkian Foundation. This foundation funds many libraries throughout Portugal and has its own excellent museum in Lisbon. Also in the square is the church from which the pousada gets its name. Nossa Senhora da Oliveira was founded by Countess Mumadona in the 10th century, largely rebuilt by João I after his victorious battle at Aljubarrota * and much modernised over the centuries. Adjoining the cloisters is the Alberto Sampaio Museum. From the square, the Rua da Rainha leads to another museum, Martins Sarmento, which will interest archaeologists. The area surrounding the adjoining Largo do Toural has several period houses, some of the ground floors of which have been converted into shops.

If you have reached saturation point with monuments, museums and the like, and none of the suggestions listed in the chapter on Guimarães' other pousada appeals to you, there is a spa at Caldas de Vizela (12 kms south on EN 105 and 106).

The chapter on the other Guimarães pousada (Santa Marinha da Costa) should be read in conjunction with these observations.

*see Pousada do Mestre Afonso Domingues, Batalha.

Top left: *Oporto on the banks of the Douro.* MK
Top right: *Oporto street market.* MK
Below: *Stairway of the Bom Jesus sanctuary.* MK

N. SRA. DE OLIVEIRA • GUIMARÃES

THE POUSADA

The pousada buildings date back to the 13th century. Originally private houses, much modified over the generations, they were aquired about 1970 and after considerable adaption opened in 1973.

The pousada got its name from the legend of King Wamba, a Visigoth, somewhere about the mid-7th century. He did not, it seems, much care for the idea of ruling and said he would only do so if the olive branch staff he was carrying sprouted when he thrust it into the ground. It did and he became King !

This lovely old hostelry is under the very experienced direction of Dona Dinorah Costa who has been on the hotel circuit for more years than she cares to remember. Increasingly she leaves the detailed running of the pousada to her daughter, Susana, and her son-in-law, José Agosto. Her other daughter, Carla, who used to run the tourist shop next door, has now opened her own restaurant, Prato Cheio, at nearby Vermoim.

There is a piquancy in some of the pousada restaurant dishes like Alascas à Pá de Piedade (pork fillet) and Entrecosto de Vitela à Cortador (veal steaks) which is explained when one knows the director's Angolan background. The menu changes daily and includes some good trout, bass and hake dishes. We have not sampled the Bacalhau à Gomes de Sá, but intend to do so on our next visit. Incidentally, this pousada produces the best buttered toast (torrada) in Portugal.

Da Oliveira has all the friendly, personal atmosphere of a family-run coaching house. Beamed ceilings, studded leather chairs, antique paintings and gentle lighting extend a warmth of welcome which comes with the years. It is lived in and loved, alive and unpretentious, but lacking nothing in comfort or cuisine. It has a lift, a tiny television room at the end of the first floor corridor and, fortunately in this conjested town centre, several reserved parking lots for guests in the square immediately adjoining the rear entrance.

HOW TO FIND

Very easy. In the centre of the historic city of Guimarães which lies 22 km south-west of Braga and 49 km north-east of Oporto.

Tel: **(053) 514157/8/9**
Fax: **(053) 514204**
Telex: **32875**

FACILITIES

GRADE

C^{Sup}

Top left: *The pousada.* E
Top right: *Pousada dining-room.* E
Centre: *Pousada bedroom.* E
Bottom left: *Guimarães castle,
"Birthplace" of Portugal.* MK

SANTA MARINHA DA COSTA • GUIMARÃES

THE AREA

It all started in this most northern province. Rightly called the cradle of Portugal, it was the birthplace of the first king of the independent country - Afonso Henriques (1139 - 1185). As if to commemorate the fact, two pousadas are available to the visitor. One here on the outskirts, and Nossa Senhora da Oliveira in the centre of the town. It is a lovely old town about which more is written on the chapter dealing with Santa Maria de Oliveira.

Whereas the neighbouring towns of Braga and Barcelos have interesting histories and buildings, Famalicão to the west is typical of the general spread of industry in this area. Textiles, wood, pottery and heavier engineering works are all necessary in an expanding and progressive economy, and their intrusion must be forgiven. By and large they are discreetly located. Santo Tirso on the river Ave is another busy textile town, but it is redeemed by a gem of Portuguese architecture - the Benedictine monastery of São Bento. It is not on everyone's itinerary because it is now used as an agricultural college and therefore private. If you ask politely you can get in, certainly to see the façade, and it is in this that the real charm of the place is encapsulated. Its classic simplicity is relieved by ornamental stone lintels over doors and windows, but Friar Turriana, who was the architect at the time of the rebuilding in 1659, knew that ornamentation alone can never put right a bad basic design. The chapel wing may disappoint but don't blame the Friar - he died in 1679 before this section was built.

The towns of Braga (22 kms) and Barcelos (44 kms) warrant a bit of time. They are easily reached via the EN 101 and 103. Braga is sometimes euphuistically called 'Portugal's Rome', presumably because of the large number of fountains and churches to be found there and the fact that the Roman Catholic Primate of Portugal is the Archbishop of Braga. It has some fine domestic architecture and like most historical towns it is best explored on foot. As good a place as any to start is the tourist office in the Praça da República where useful advice can be obtained. Have a look at the 16th-century Casa dos Crivos, the Archbishop's Palace, the cathedral, the 14th-century King's Chapel and the 17th-century mansion, Casa dos Biscainhos. The local councillors have done themselves well in the Praça do Município and another fine building is the ornate Casa do Mexicano (or Palácio do Raio). On the outskirts, Bom Jesus is a much visited church. Whether the steps are worth climbing is a matter of personal choice. Even from the bottom it is an impressive sight. Wax candles are a good buy in Braga.

Barcelos is another ancient town. The outskirts, with developments like the hideous, high-rise Santa Clara complex and the scattering of industrial buildings in all directions, are inclined to put off most people. Persevere if only to track down the home of the Cock of Barcelos which has now become, thanks to good PR work by local tradesmen, the national emblem - as it is in France. There are all sorts of variations, but the central theme of the legend is the same. In the 14th century a criminal, sentenced to death, vehemently proclaimed his innocence. He told the

5

SANTA MARINHA DA COSTA • GUIMARÃES

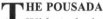

judge that to prove it, a cock would crow. That night at dinner, the judge was about to carve his chicken when the bird let forth a 'cock-a-doodle-do' of such sincerity, he ordered the prisoner's release. In the museum of the former Ducal Palace is some statuary erected, it is claimed, by the released prisoner. A pinch of salt with your chicken might be the order of the day, but the legend has provided the opportunity for local factories to produce gaudy coloured cockrels by the millions. The tourist office in the ancient Torre de Menagem has more cockrels in every conceivable size than it has literature. The Thursday market in Campo de Feira da República, is one of the largest in Portugal.

Previous page: *Pousada interior E*
Opposite and below: *The pousada. E/SR*

THE POUSADA

Without doubt, this is one of the most fabulous jewel in the already glittering crown of Portuguese pousadas.

Santa Marinha da Costa opened its doors to an expectant public on 2nd August 1985. Absolutely palatial, it is the biggest and by far the most impressive of all the pousadas in Portugal, and unrivalled on the Iberian peninsula. It has to be seen to be believed. It takes time to absorb it all. Just when you think the layout has been mastered, from the reception area through the tiled and sunken bar and lounge to the vaulted dining room, you discover that much remains. There are discreet cloisters, the São Jerónimo fountain at the end of the fantastically long bedroom corridor is where, it is rumoured, Senhor Leite de Castro, the last private owner, exercised his horse. The ante-room is decorated with 16th century azulejos (wall tiles) by Policarpo Oliveira Bernardes and then, as if the foregoing was not enough, the enormous and sumptuously furnished drawing-room of about 240 square metres awaits you. There are 55 bedrooms, two suites, lift, air-conditioning and central heating. The whole is set in wooded grounds of 12 hectares (30 acres).

The earliest written evidence concerning the site was in 959 AD when in the will of Mumadona the property 'Lourosa' was left to the Monastery of Guimarães. There is a Praça de Mumadona adjoining the Ducal Palace of Bragança at the junction of Rua Serpa Pinto and Rua D. Constança de Noronha. There is little doubt that Lourosa included Santa Marinha da Costa and that Queen Mafalda, wife of King Afonso Henriques, established a

religous order for the canons of St Augustine. In 1528 the Duke of Bragança obtained the Pope's authorisation to establish a monastery for the monks of São Jerónimo, and it seems probable António Crato received his education here. He was the last of the Grand Priors of a branch of the Knights Hospitallers. Before dying in Paris in 1595, he made a couple of attempts (in 1581 and 1589) to claim the Portuguese throne. In 1834 many lands belonging to the church were secularised and Santa Marinha da Costa passed to Dom António de Araujo Fernandes Leite de Castro. At the same time it was designated as a building of national importance, which it remains today. Later, the Jesuits occupied the monastery until the buildings were devastated by a major fire in 1951. Thereafter the Leite de Castro family lived in the rambling and deteriorating mansion until it was aquired for conversion to a pousada in 1975. The chief architect, Fernando Tavora, deserves our congratulations and thanks for halting the further deterioration of this historic building and utilising his skills in bringing Santa Marinha da Costa into the 20th century.

When the pousada first opened, the food was not up to the standard of the building in which it was served. There was no à la carte menu and although the set menu was adequately cooked it lacked imagination. There was a museum-like atmosphere in which flowers, ticking clocks and the sound of laughter were missing. The crown of Santa Marinha sat precariously and self-consciously on her head.

Now, a few years later, it is a very different place. Time and good management have produced a reputation for good food and service. Tradition is not created overnight.

There is an extensive à la carte to satisfy every taste. Among the dishes sampled on our last stay were Figos com Presunto (smoked ham with figs), Cocktail de Pêra Abacate (avocado cocktail, Salmão Estufado com Alho (salmon with garlic) and Açorda de Bacalhau (cooked salted cod with bread pap and herbs. The wine list has 84 offerings. Lello 1987 Reserva was the wine recommended and it was good. On a Monday evening in November

HOW TO FIND

Needs care. From Guimarães take the small road to Penha (east of Guimarães) EN101. After 2 kms, at Costa, take a small road to the left leading to the pousada, which is next door to the church.

Tel: **(053) 514453/4/5/6/7**
Fax: **(053) 514459** Telex: **32686**

FACILITIES

GRADE

there were 42 people in the dining-room and the head waiter told us that altogether he had served 61 dinners. Reserve a table.

Plans for tennis courts and a swimming pool have been delayed but there is a good public pool adjoining the grounds. There is plenty of car parking, including some covered spaces adjoining the open forecourt.

The pousada. SR

SÃO BARTOLOMEU • BRAGANÇA

THE AREA

Bragança is the most north-easterly town in Portugal, over 500 kms from Lisbon and only 30 kms from Spain. The Parque Nacional de Montesinho, which lies immediately to the north, can be explored on foot or by car and from it, on a clear day, the sun shines on the distant snow-capped mountains of Spains's Sierra de la Cabrera (2200 metres). To the south, the town is protected by the Serra da Nogueira.

Due largely to poor communications, this area has remained aloof from the rest of Portugal. Whether staying in Bragança or at the other Trás-os-Montes pousada at Miranda do Douro there is this feeling of isolation. It is a land of mystery and myth where, in the past, minorities have taken up residence to avoid persecution. Jewish refugees from the Inquisition came to settle and as recently as 1927 their descendents opened a synagogue. Modern motorways linking Bragança to Vila Real and Oporto are making access easier, but hopefully will not dispel the haunting atmosphere of this lonely backwater. Many of the carefully preserved rites and festivals celebrated in these parts are more pagan than Christian. The masks worn by the children and the not so young, between Christmas day and 6th Janurary (12th night in England - 'Day of the Kings' in Portugal) are pretty horrendous.

The guidebooks do not do justice to this province. It is as though the compilers found it too isolated and not worth the trouble of researching. There is a lot to discover in this fascinatingly different part of Portugal and, with the aid of a knowledgeable local resident, it is an interesting story to unfold.

There are so many nearby villages and hamlets to see that the visitor need never be at a loose end. Take the EN 103 to ancient Vinhais, not forgetting en route to inspect the strange and disintegrating monanstery of Castro de Avelãs (5 kms). In Vinhais there are several houses of note and the 17th century fountain in the Largo do Arrabalde, bearing the coat of arms of the Count of Arrabalde, is charming. On the other side of Bragança the EN 308 and 218 lead to Gimonde with its Roman bridge, and Outeiro whose Santo Cristo church and Gothic pillory make a rewarding excursion. Izeda, to the south of the pousada on EN 217 (40 kms) is another fascinating old town.

In Bragança itself the 12th century castle, the original seat of the ruling Braganças, is surrounded by well tended gardens. Probably the most interesting building is the medieval Domus Municipalis. This town hall on Roman foundations is not keen on showing its charm to the visitor, but the key can be obtained. Ask at the tourist office if it is not open. The Princess tower of the castle and the old cathedral both have early pillories nearby. Also within the ramparts is the castle church of Santa Maria. The Museum of Abade de Baçal is located in the former Bishop's Palace. The church of São Vincente is reputedly where King Pedro married his lover. *

see Batalha pousada for the lovers' story

Opposite page: Bragança castle at dawn and sunset. MK

SÃO BARTOLOMEU • BRAGANÇA

THE POUSADA

The pousada celebrated its 25th anniversary in 1984 and the special velvet bound and embroidered guest book for that year shows how wide is its appeal. Signatures of professors from Switzerland, doctors from St. Bartholemew's Hospital in London and visitors from New York, Germany, Denmark and elsewhere make interesting reading.

There will be no cause to complain of the food at São Bartolomeu. Trout and game in season from local sources are well presented. Although the menu is limited, it changes daily; there is much to be said for restricted, well-cooked dishes rather than a mile-long but indifferent offering. Feijoada à Transmontana (beans and pork) may not be most people's idea of haute cuisine but it is a very typical dish of Portugal. There is always a good home-made soup available and wines to suit all tastes. With a light lunch, Tuela Seco wine is most enjoyable.

The decor is dominated by matured wood and natural stone. The only suggested improvement might be the substitution of the stark ceiling lights with something more sophisticated. The perforated metal standard lamps fit in well. The pousada encourages local residents from the town and the presence of the youth of Bragança adds to the atmosphere. Apart from the automatic switch-on of the television, without which as background accompaniment the youth of today seem unable to converse, they are a cheery, well-behaved and attractive crowd.

The service throughout is good. The bedrooms are spacious with a view of the floodlit castle on the other side of the small valley. Sadly, an increasing number of high-rise apartment blocks has done little to enhance the view. There is good car parking with six lock-up garages.

Bragança may be approached either by the EN 15 and IP 4 from Vila Real (138 kms) or the more northerly EN 103 via Chaves (65 kms). Both have spectacular mountain scenery and if it is possible to make a circular tour, do so. If you leave on the southern route stop off at Romeu, a small village on the south of the road before Mirandela. Restored by government and private funds 45 years ago, it possess Maria Rita's delightful restaurant and a

HOW TO FIND

Straightforward. On the outskirts of Bragança (in Portugal's most north-easterly corner) coming from Vila Real (south-west). The pousada is in the Estrada do Turismo, on the right.

Tel: **(073) 331493/494**
Fax: **(073) 23453** Telex: **22613**

FACILITIES

RECREATION

GRADE

tiny museum alongside. 11,000 square metres of roof were renewed in the restoration of this dying village. The local benefactor was José Menéres, a port wine king. But this is for tomorrow. Take your glass to the terrace of the pousada and look across at the castle of the Braganças. History is looking back at you.

Top: *Celebrating the Festa dos Rapazes.* MK
Centre: *Pousada terrace.* E
Bottom right: *Inside the castle.* MK

SANTA CATARINA • MIRANDA DO DOURO

THE AREA

Trás-os-Montes (beyond the mountains) is an area of remote charm. Because of its remoteness several customs have survived longer than in the more accessible middle and southern parts of the country. A sort of Latin slang, known as Mirandês, is still heard in the villages. It is equally common to find, even in the remotest hamlet, a French or German-speaking Portuguese family who have returned from earning a good salary overseas.

There are many local customs and legends whose origins are lost in the mists of time. One concerns Miranda do Douro's 16th-century cathedral in which little Jesus is the proud possessor of a top hat! Legend has it that a young lad enthusiastically urged his seniors to resist the Spanish invaders. Spurred on by his shouts of encouragement, they were successful. Despite the fact that the young lad disappeared after the battle, the town wished to honour the event. A statuette was made of young Jesus surmounted, not by a crown of thorns, but by a top hat.

Another custom centred around the cathedral occurs on Christmas day. It is called 'Fogueira do galo' (Christmas bonfire) - 'Missa do galo' is Christmas midnight mass. The young bachelors of the town are directed by an anually elected council of six senior citizens to collect a mountain of firewood in carts and deposit it in the churchyard. In front of the ensuing blaze the folk of Miranda gather - it can be bitterly cold at this time of the year. Failure to discharge their task conscientiously results in a fine - payable in wine. There is much merriment and the batchelor of this year may well meet his bride of next year. Nobody knows how long this tradition has been in existence.

Yet another custom surviving the centuries is the Pauliteiros Dance performed on the third Sunday in August. The Pauliteiros is a kind of sword-fight with sticks, accompanied by the rhythm of tambourines and bagpipes. Don't confuse it with *paliteiro* - a toothpick holder.

People from these parts are proud and independent. They have a rhyming legend in Trás-os-Montes: 'P'ra cá do Marão mandam os que cá estão, e p'ra lá mandarão ou não'. Roughly translated it means: 'We on this side of the mountains of Marão (the southern boundary of Trás-os-Montes) are rulers; on the other side not necessarily so. Remember, the House of Bragança (Trás-os-Montes) ruled Portugal from 1640 to the end of the monarchy in 1910.

The countryside between Miranda do Douro and Bragança is often reminiscent of parts of Britain. There is little traffic on the secondary roads, which adds to the sense of remoteness. Along the roadside are cherry trees and wild dog roses. Agriculture is more productive than it used to be because of the modern machinery purchased by itinerant Portuguese workers. The pockets of vines increase as Miranda do Douro is approached. There are a few large fields of corn, but in the main it is the ever changing character that impresses - here an orchard, there a clump of pines and a few small fields of vegetables, particularly on the outskirts of rare and scattered villages. White marble and wolfram are local products.

The inverted horses' hoof-like buildings puzzled us. They are dotted about

in no particular pattern. After enquiring, we discovered they are pigeon lofts. They do not seem greatly used nowadays because there are no pigeons. In past days, when a holding was divided between inheriting children, the one who came by the pigeon-loft was often better off than those inheriting the house !

It is suggested that these notes are read in conjunction with the chapter on the pousada São Bartolomeu at Bragança.

Top left: *The Christ child with a top hat.* MK
Top right: *The dam.* MK
Centre: *The village of Mazouco.* MK
Bottom right: *Trás-os-Montes pigeon loft.* SR

SANTA CATARINA • MIRANDA DO DOURO

THE POUSADA
Perched on the edge of the rocky gorge of the Barragem of Miranda do Douro, this pousada was originally built in connection with a joint Portuguese and Spanish government project to establish a chain of dams along the Douro to provide hydro-electric power. It was subsequently adapted and opened as a pousada in 1962. A road now runs across the dam the centre of which is the boundary between the two countries. It can be seen from the bedrooms and public rooms of the pousada. It is an unforgettable view. The agitated flow of this long, natural river running from Oporto right across Portugal and deep into Spain has been tamed and harnessed by the skill of engineers to form a peaceful lake. Vultures wheel in the sky. Gulls appear like confetti on the waters below. With luck you may see a golden eagle. Bird identification books at the ready, it is a great spot for ornithologists.

From the terrace there is the feeling you can almost touch Spain on the other side of this sheer, rock-faced gorge. It is interesting to try to pick out which is Portugal and which is Spain as the river interlaces the ravines. Like a maze, it is more difficult than you would think.

The sense of being able to reach across to make contact with Spain was acknowledged by Wellington. When wishing to visit his troops in Portugal, he decided the quickest way was to be winched across the ravine. The year was 1813. The great soldier had already proved himself a man of exceptional military perspicacity. He must also have had an exceptional head for heights !

Public rooms and bedrooms are spacious and there is a very good terrace from which to enjoy this impressive and unique outlook.

Although restricted, the menu changes daily and is freshly cooked by a local woman. She enjoys cooking, often preferring to exercise her skills over a wood fire. The soups are, as you would expect in Portugal, first rate. There are usually three fish and three meat dishes on offer. Guisado de Polvo à Transmontana (octopus ragout) is one of many excellent specialities. Another typical winter dish is Alheiras Mirandela (a smoked bread and meat sausage with a fried egg). Originally

HOW TO FIND
Easy. In the centre of Miranda do Douro. In the Estrada da Barragem (the road to the lake), on the left, next to the branch of the Banco Português do Atlântico (BPA).

Tel: **(073) 41005/255**
Fax: **(073) 41065** Telex. **22388**

FACILITIES

RECREATION

GRADE

it was made of pork, but as Trás-os-Montes became the home of Jews persecuted in other parts, the pork was dropped in preference for other meat. Quince jam is traditional and often eaten with cheese. The wines from Sendim (about 20 kms) are local. Vallepradinhos, Tuela and Valpaos are all good, either in white or red, and so too are the wines from Val Flor (south of Mirandela) which also produces a decent cheese.

When writing the first edition of this guide, wines from Trás-os-Montes were not demarcated, although they deserved to be. They are now, largely to obtain grants available through the European Community.

Santa Catarina hasn't the casual passing trade of the more centrally located pousadas. By and large travellers don't happen to be in Miranda do Douro by chance; they have made a special journey. The area has a growing appeal. The more often you visit it, the more attractive you find it. There is always a warm welcome from the people of these parts, and none warmer and more sincere than from Dona Maria de Jesus and the staff at Santa Catarina.

Above: *The pousada.* E

BARÃO FORRESTER • ALIJÓ

THE AREA

It would be difficult after a stay at this pousada not to have acquired an interest and knowledge, however eclectic, in the production of port wine. Take the steep Pinhão road from Alijó (EN 322) and, after crossing the bridge, follow the southern bank of the Douro to Régua. This is the heartland of port. On the terraced hills, climbing steeply from the river, are the port wine *quintas* with some familiar names painted on them: Sandeman, Noval, Fonseca, Offley, Quinta das Carvalhas of the Real Companhia Velha, Croft's Quinta da Roeda and, upstream, Quinta do Vesuvio, owned by the Ferreira family, Warre's Quinta do Bonfim, Quinta do Infantado and many others. While walking or motoring along the river bank you may see a *rabelo*, one of those shallow-draughted boats with a single sail, which, with the aid of a skilled navigator and a huge oar, brought the port wine barrels down river to Vila Nova de Gaia, opposite Oporto. Here in the warehouses of the major shippers, the secrets (or some of them) of the port trade may be unravelled. Many of them stage an illustrated lecture and offer a glass of their product. Here, for sure, the *rabelos* can be seen on the river. Once a year there is a race of these old craft. Tradition dies hard. With the coming of the railway most of the wine was moved by train from Régua; now it is mostly done by road. The Casa do Douro in Régua houses the Instituto do Vinho do Porto which, in addition to a good, modern, stained glass window depicting the wine harvest, can give any information the peripatetic student may require. The thing that surprises most visitors is the ground in which the vines grow. Slatey and barren with no humus, it looks as though it couldn't succor a rapacious weed.

Perhaps the good living of the 19th century with its incidence of gout and obesity prompted Prime Minister Pombal, the architect of much of modern Portugal, to initiate the construction of the spa at nearby Moledo. Certainly in 1756, his brainchild resulted in the formation of Companhia Geral da Agricultura das Vinhas do Alto Douro, which today is known as Real Companhia Velha. Its vinho espumante, natural brut, metodo champanhês is an excellent drink. It may not be French champagne, but it is a good substitute at a fraction of the price. Try it.

Lamego is only 15 kms south of Régua and if a predilection for port can be overcome, a visit is rewarding. The Sanctuary of our Lady of Redemption with its 286 steps is very much like the Bom Jesus at Braga and from it there is a fine view of the town and surrounding country. Lamego is renowned for its pottery and there are good examples of decorative tiles on several buildings.

Below: *A local farmer's welcoming smile.* MK

Top: *Harvesting the grapes.* MK
Centre: *Port wine country.* MK
Bottom left: *A rabelo in festive rig.* MK

BARÃO FORRESTER • ALIJÓ

THE POUSADA
After being substantially redeveloped, this pousada opened again in 1983. Although fronting the road and next door to the Post Office of the pleasant but uninspiring little town of Alijó, it has restful views at the rear across vineyards and countryside.

The name Barão Forrester is part of the history of port wine. As a young man, James Forrester (1809 - 1862) came to work in his uncle's firm, Offley Forrester and Co. By all accounts he was a gifted man who, unlike some of his compatriots, mastered the language and integrated into Portuguese society. He was an artist and a cartographer. A copy of his map of the Douro is on one of the pousada's walls. He was a purist in his desire to keep port as a wine unfortified by brandy (a battle he eventually lost) and he was instrumental in eradicating the use of elderberries for colouring.

There is a central dining-room, with mirrored doors on both sides, a *sala* (drawing-room) and on the lower garden level, a card room and modern bar with an unrivalled collection of old ports. Twenty-three are listed, including a 25-year-old Offley. Port of this quality, particularly by the glass, is not cheap. Your hostess, Dona Maria do Carmo Lemos, knows about port and is only too happy, particularly outside the very busy summer months, to arrange a visit to a quinta.

The food is good and varied. The waiter on our last visit was Joaquim Carvalho and he went to a lot of bother to prepare a table on the terrace out of the sun. It was an excellent light lunch; a prawn omelet (the Portuguese don't seem able to make a bad one) followed by fresh melon with a glass of port added to the juice. The white wine was from the local co-operativa, beautifully chilled and relaxing on a particularly hot day. Specialities are their bacalhau (dried salted cod) and pickled peixinhos (little river fish apparently with no other name and a dish not met on other menus). On the wine front there is no need to venture outside those on the doorstep. Adega Co-operativa de Alijó produces good wine. The *reservas* are recommended despite their higher price, but the Granja is very drinkable.

It requires some will-power not to

HOW TO FIND
Easy. In the town of Alijó, next door to the Post Office (Correio). To get to Alijó take the road from Vila Real to Bragança. Some kilometres before Murça, a road to the right leads south to Alijó.
Tel: **(059) 959215**
Fax: **(059) 959304** Telex: **26364**

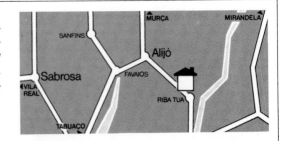

FACILITIES

RECREATION

GRADE

follow meals with a glass of port, and chilled white port as an aperitif is the next step in the progression, or retrogression. If port is not for you, Alijó produces a good and fruity moscatel which is not widely known. It is every bit as good as the demarcated 'Moscatel de Setúbal'.

There is a model of a *rabelo* from which, on 12th May 1862, Forrester fell and was drowned but not before he had been created a Baron by the King of Portugal, an honour also bestowed on an earlier merchant, John Croft, who was given the title Barão de Estrela.

Recent improvements to this progressive pousada include the addition of a swimming pool and, adjoining it, a tennis court. The car parking has also been improved.

Top left: *In the pousada gardens. SR*
Top right: *The pousada. E*
Centre: *The meandering Douro. MK*

SÃO GONÇALO • SERRA DO MARÃO

THE AREA

Although the new east-west IP 4 has greatly increased the accessibility of these forested mountains, the pousada still retains the welcoming atmosphere of an isolated retreat. It provides a good central location for exploring the area and the towns on either side - Amarante and Vila Real.

Amarante is an ancient town which has developed at a crossing of the river Tâmega. Dominating the town and looking down regally on the river is the convent and church of São Gonçalo. It is an imposing and aesthetically pleasing 16th-century building in which the local saint, Gonçalo, is buried. The tomb must have been moved there as the convent had not yet been founded in the 13th century when he died. Gonçalo is the patron saint of lovers and it is claimed that husband-seekers may be certain of marrying within the year if they rub their naked flesh against his tomb. To increase the chances of matrimony, a Bolinho de Amor might just do the trick. This is a sponge-cake, baked in phallic form and offered during the first weekend of June - a custom probably dating back to a pre-Christian fertility cult. The *Blue Guide to Portugal* tells us that Gonçalo's "erection collapsed in 1763" (referring to the bridge). It seems doubtful,therefore, whether the spell of tomb and sponge-cake will be as efficacious as was hoped !

There are several riverside cafes from which to enjoy the view. The town was damaged by French troops in 1809 and there is a plaque on the lovely bridge (1790) honouring those who died in defence of their homeland.

Vila Real, 23 kms in the other direction from the pousada, is a prosperous town. Mateus Rosé, with its world-famous label picturing the Palácio de Mateus, is produced there by Sogrape. Beautifully presented in its flagon-type bottle, it is a masterpiece of clever marketing if not of the viniculturist's art. Raymond Postgate, the wine buff, describes a rosé wine drinker as either a drunk or a shareholder in the company selling it - a little unkind considering 55 million bottles are exported annually. There must be a host of drunken shareholders staggering around the 150 countries importing it ! The palace on the eastern outskirts of the town is the country home of the Count of Vila Real. It is open to the public and, even if it is a trifle too baroque for those with unornamented classical taste, its lakeside setting reduces the excesses and produces a distinctive and acceptable whole. The characteristic style of the 18th-century architect Nicolau Nasoni can also be evidenced in the Capela Nova in the town.

Felgueiras (not to be confused with the spa south of Viseu) is on the Amarante-Guimarães EN 101. It is a smaller, ancient town producing a less erotic sponge-cake by the name of Margaride, and some delicate lacework.

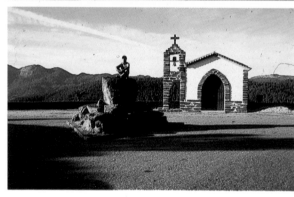

Top: *Casa de Mateus, which is pictured on the Mateus Rosé label, and its gardens.* SR MK
Centre: *Amarante, west of the pousada.* MK
Bottom left: *Chapel near Amarante.* SR

SÃO GONÇALO • SERRA DO MARÃO

THE POUSADA In the mountains of Marão and opened in 1942, with more recent modifications and improvements, this is a simple, homely pousada with a reputation for good food.

The immediate area of fir forest was destroyed in the summer of 1985 by one of the worst forest fires ever to break out in these mountains. Six hundred firemen fought the blaze. Visitors, however, may take comfort in the knowledge that lightening, bombs and forest fires never devastate the same area twice. Certainly, on the night of 16th September 1985, the godly Saint Gonçalo came to the rescue of those staying at his pousada. The patron saint, ably assisted by the fire-fighting services *(bombeiros voluntários)*, arrested the fire on the pousada's doorstep. When the evacuated guests returned, not even a stone had been charred. All around, however, was destruction. Management and guests gave a meal of bacalhau and thanks to about one hundred of the more local firemen. What a wonderfully unostentàtious job these volunteers do. Now, once again, this beautiful lonely landscape is green again. It is surprising how quickly the bloom returns to areas damaged by even the worst fires.

The menu is now in three languages with an à la carte section including such fish dishes as Truta do Rio Ovelha Recheadas com Presunto (grilled trout inserted with a slice of smoked ham). Remove the ham and the subtle, smokey taste it imparts makes the trout a wonderfully succulent dish. There are a couple of bacalhau dishes, one of which formed the basis of the firmen's spread in 1985. Do try to persevere with bacalhau (dried and salted cod). There are so many ways of preparing it (one for each day of the year, they say) that sooner or later you will hit on one that justifies the previous and perhaps disappointing experiments. Polvo de Caldeirada (octopus stew) is again not to everyone's liking at first encounter, but it is a typical Portuguese dish and will grow on you if washed down by a good vinho verde like Moura Basto or Quinta do Outeiro de Baixo. Coelho à Transmontana (rabbit from Trás-os-Montes) and Caldeirada de Cabrito à Serrana (stewed kid) are both good. The beef is better than usual in a country where

HOW TO FIND

Easy. Off the main road IP4 from Oporto to Vila Real, about midway between Amarante (24 kms) and Vila Real (20 kms).

Tel: **(055) 461113/23/4**
Fax: **(055) 461353** Telex: **26321**

FACILITIES

GRADE

B

other choices are often more prudent. Chateaubriand and Tornedos Rossini are on the menu. The latter, in addition to a slice of flavoured toast, includes ham capped by an omlette.

The wine list has an inovation which could well be copied in all the pousadas. A number are marked with 'R' which might suggest it was a 'reserva', but the 'R' here simply means it is a local (region) wine. Vinho verde São Gonçalo, São Gonçalo Tinto, and Santa Marta are three so marked. There are also the wines from Vila Real which go well with the fairly rich menu. In the past we thought the chef a bit heavy-handed with the salt, but this is perhaps more to the Portuguese taste. Papos de Anjo (angel's breasts) is a well-known

local sweet and rather less exciting than it sounds.

With good central heating from old-fashioned hospital type radiators, which seem to throw out more heat than any of their concealed successors, it is a cosy place even in winter, despite its 885 metres height. Because of its proximity to the business centre of Vila Real, the pousada is more in demand than would seem likely - particularly at weekends. It is a warm comfortable hostelry in winter and a cool mountain retreat in the summer.

Above: *The pousada.* E

53

SENHORA DAS NEVES • ALMEIDA

THE AREA

Close to Spain, this is an area which is not much on the tourist map. Partly for that reason it has a feeling of remoteness which is accentuated in the wild and rocky Serra de Marofa.

Guarda, the capital of the province of Beira Alta, lies some 60 kms to the south-west and at 1000 metres is the highest major town in Portugal. Of the three 'Beiras', Beira Alta is the highest. 'Beira' means edge or side of (beira-mar = seaside). Beira Litoral (near the sea) and Beira Baixa (the lowlands) are the smaller neighbouring provinces. Rather like Trás-os-Montes, described in earlier chapters, Beira Alta is not the guide compiler's favourite hunting ground. It is a bit off the beaten track and, apart from the towns of Viseu and Guarda, does not seem to warrant their attention. *Fodor's Guide*, excellent in so many ways, doesn't even mention Almeida. More's the pity, because for many visitors this may be where the first night in Portugal is spent.

Crossing the frontier at Vilar Formoso it is tempting to push on along the fast new trunk road IP 5 to the west. Resist the temptation. Make a 10 kms diversion to the north and stay at Almeida. Hopefully your schedule will allow time enough to have a look at the immediate surroundings - if only to see the storks. Wherever there are storks there is water. Here the river Côa and a number of smaller tributaries provide irrigation to a flourishing, verdant valley of vines, olives, almond, fruit and vegetables.

Malpartida only a few kilometres north-east on a minor undesignated road is a border village where, two years before the fortress of Almeida fell, the French were engaged in battle. It produces a very strong but rather dry cheese. Time permitting, continue on this minor road to Figueira de Castelo Rodrigo where, as in so many of these walled border towns, there are the ruins of a castle originally constructed by King Dinis (1279 -1325). The return journey can be made on EN 221, forking left in Pinhel to the EN 324. A speedier return can be made by omitting Pinhel and returning on the EN 322.

South of the IP 5, the village of Malhada Sorda shows the influence of the invading Arabs in its domestic architecture and ancient methods of drawing water. Here, a dying cottage industry is carried on in the manufacture of pottery - every piece is slightly different. The machine may be perfect, but the hands of the local ladies produce something hallmarked with personality and pride.

This is an area which should not be missed if travelling at the end of February and March when the blossom on almond and other fruit trees is at its best. The written word could not do justice to its loveliness.

Top left: *A Serra da Estrela stream in springtime.* MK
Top right: *The pousada is within strong fortifications.* MK
Below: *The frontier at sunset.* SR

SENHORA DAS NEVES • ALMEIDA

THE POUSADA
Almeida is a fortress town but not commercialised as many are. Like most of these fortified towns it has been around for a long time and during its history has changed hands between the Portuguese, Spanish and French. King Dinis conquered the town in 1296 and made it part of Portugal the following year. During subsequent reigns it was extended and improved. The present star-shaped lay-out owes much to that doyen of military defences, the Frenchman Marshal Sebastien de Vauban (1633 - 1707). During the wars of Louis XIV he was responsible for over one hundred fortresses. Not surprisingly his geometric star-shaped design with a moat became the accepted standard - largely because the lay-out enabled enfiladed artillery fire to be used effectively.

Almeida is immortalised in the history of the Peninsula Wars. Wellington's forces were under siege from the French. Barrels of gunpowder were being transferred to the ramparts. A French bomb landed close to the fort doors and ignited a trail of gunpowder which had leaked from a split barrel. The gunpowder acted as a fuse running down to the main magazine in the cellars. One minute later, the whole of Almeida erupted. The most violent explosion the world had seen obliterated the town on the 26th August 1810. The cathedral and surrounding houses were reduced to rubble. It was reported that the noise of the explosion, which killed an estimated 1,300, was heard more than 50 kms away.

Now all is peaceful and serene. The dust has long since settled. The delightfully named pousada (Our Lady of the Snows) offers the traveller the opportunity of making a rendezvous with history in the comfort of a modern establishment which was opened in 1987.

Rather sensibly the restaurant menu indicates the local dishes. They include Bacalhau à Beira Alta (this salted dried cod is prepared in the oven with a Serra cheese covering), Carneiro à Moda de Fornos de Algodres (braised lamb in local red wine), Bifes de Presunto à Moda da Beira (smoked ham steak fried and marinated in white wine), Lingua de Vitela à Beira (casseroled veal tongue with ceps).

HOW TO FIND
Easy. Inside the old and small fortress town of Almeida which lies close to the Spanish frontier west-north-west of Guarda and south-west of Pinhel.

Tel: **(071) 54283/90**
Fax: **(071) 54320** Telex: **52713**

FACILITIES

RECREATION

GRADE

The pousada. SR/E

The restaurant also offers good flambé dishes which some may consider a little ostentatious in their presentation. Be that as it may, the Lombo de Porco em Vermute com Laranja (tenderloin of pork in vermouth and orange) is very good indeed. Among the starters, Espadarte de Sesimbra Fumado (smoked swordfish) and Espetadinha de Mexilhão à Pescador (mussels kebab with vinagrette dressing) are tasty and perhaps a little less usual than the normal run of hors-d'oeuvres. This pousada has an exceptional pastry chef whose sweet trolley usually tempts with some sinfully delicious offering.

The wines from nearby Pinhel deserve better recognition; the red table wine from the area is good value. Of the local wines, Dom Manuel I Reserva is one of the more expensive. There is a comprehensive list which includes some expensive wines from over the border and from France. Marquis de Souveral Garrafeira (estate selected and bottled) is as good as any.

When it was originally opened, this pousada was given the top grading of Chateau. It is now category C. The decor lacks imagination and more could be made of the illustrious past. What it lacks is compensated by an exceptionally helpful and courteous staff. The bedrooms are spacious with some silk embroidery panels which, at a guess, were worked in Castelo Branco. A number of the bedrooms have verandahs with commanding views.

One very good reason for staying at Almeida is the underground car park. Often cars leaving Portugal are laden to the gunwales with as much wine and other goods as conscience and customs permit and it is good to relax over dinner in the knowledge that there is no risk of pilfering. In fact, since the pousada opened there has been no incidence of theft. When leaving or entering Portugal, the traveller says 'Goodbye' with regret and 'Hello' with real pleasure.

RIA • RIA DE AVEIRO

THE AREA

Aveiro, with just under 30,000 inhabitants, is an interesting city with a museum in the Convent of Jesus, salt-flats, and some good classical houses overlooking the canals.

The area is well-known for its production of ceramics including *azulejos,* glazed tiles so named because *azul,* meaning blue, was their predominant colour. Good examples of this art can be seen in such streets as Rua de João Mendonça, Rua de Barbosa de Magalhães and Rua do Rato in Aveiro. There is a tourist office in the Praça da República from which you can obtain a street plan and helpful literature. The porcelain works of Vista Alegre, renowned both in Portugal and overseas, have their headquarters and an interesting museum near Ílhavo, a short run south of the town.

At one time the port of Aveiro was busy and prosperous. The silting up of the entrance to the harbour by deposits brought down by the river Vouga, combined with a build-up of sand from the sea, meant that by the end of the 17th century, following some exceptionally rough seas, the port was landlocked. In 1808 a successful attempt was made to pierce an entrance in the sand-bar, but it is unlikely that Aveiro will ever become a major port again. Dock works are going on, but they are near the entrance at São Jacinto where the shipyards and air base are located.

On the inland waterways you will notice the distinctive and pretty *moliceiros*. These shallow-draught boats, originally propelled by a squarish gaff-rigged sail but more often today by an outboard engine, are very much part of the local scene. With their high, painted bow and stern, they have been partly responsible for Aveiro's pseudonym: the Venice of Portugal. However, these boats carry, not romantic singing gondoliers, but algae which is used as a fertiliser.

Exploration of the surrounding areas has been made much easier by the construction of new north-south and east-west motorways. Two excursions that suggest themselves: out on the RN 109 to Figueira da Foz; turn inland there to follow the north bank of the river Mondego via Montemor-o-Velho and Tentúgal. If Aveiro is the Venice of Portugal, Figueira da Foz is certainly its Blackpool ! The return can either be by the fast A1 or, if the university town of Coimbra is to be included, back on the old E 50 via Anadia and Águeda. Curia, on the way home, is a spa so saturated with the spirit and atmosphere of the belle époque that a brief pause there is an experience. The second trip follows the north bank of the Vouga through Oliveira de Frades to Viseu and then home on the fast IP 5. There are many things to see on this route including some beautiful riverside scenery.

Opposite: *Brightly painted moliceiros.* MK
Below: *Aveiro.* MK

THE POUSADA
A glance at the map will explain why an approach through the town of Aveiro is not recommended. Aveiro possesses, among its other charms, the prettiest policewomen in Portugal. The fact that they have but a passing aquaintance with the Pousada da Ria and absolutely no idea of how to get there, is surprisingly easily forgiven.

This pousada dips its toes into the sheltered lagoon waters of Ria de Aveiro. It has been a popular retreat since it opened in 1960 with nine bedrooms. Another nine bedrooms were added in 1985 and the teething troubles with supplying hot water to them have been overcome. The swimming pool has been modernised and a tennis court constructed in the grounds. The bedrooms are large and well-appointed. They and the reception rooms look out across the water.

Eels, from the sheltered waters of Ria de Aveiro, form the basis of a couple of specialities - Caldeirada de Enguias (an eel stew or chowder) and Enguias de Escabeche (marinated eels). Quite a few people can't stand eels in any form, and for them there are plenty of other choices. Rojões (pork cubes, crisped and sautéed) is one. The food in general is imaginative with local and slightly different dishes included. For wines, look no further than those from Bairrada which, surpringly enough, was not a demarcated region until 1979. The Messias and Alianças in white or red are good value - but all the Bairradas are pretty reliable. The '85 reds are excellent; the whites should be drunk young. Before leaving this pousada, a tidy, well-run ship with a friendly crew, walk across the isthmus and compare the might of the open Atlantic with the sheltered peacefulness of the lagoon.

Below: ***The pousada.*** E
Opposite top: ***The pousada.*** SR
Bottom: ***Aveiro, "Portugal's Venice".*** MK

HOW TO FIND

Not easy. Ignore Murtosa in the address. Take the road from Aveiro going north to Estarreja. From Estarreja take the road going west to Torreira. Then go south towards S. Jacinto. After about 3kms, a track on your left leads to the pousada beside the inland water.

Tel: **(034) 48332/4**
Fax: **(034) 48333** Telex: **37061**

FACILITIES

RECREATION

GRADE

SANTO ANTÓNIO • SERÉM

THE AREA

The valley of the river Vouga, about 10 kms north of Águeda, may not provide spectacular scenery, but it possesses a gentleness and greeness which is both restful and refreshing. The pousada is only 25 kms east of Aveiro and much that has been written under the chapter on the Pousada da Ria is applicable here at Serém. A stay at Santo António provides the opportunity of exploring not only the Vouga valley, but the several other rivers of the area. There are four of them - the Alfusqueiro, Águeda, Cértima and Levira. The last two flow into the Pateira de Fermentelos (RN 333 from Águeda), a large lake which is lovely at any time of the year, but particularly so when the water-lilies are out in the Spring. Although the area has been developed by workers returning to their native soil from overseas employment, the traditonal crafts are still carried on. Rushes growing alongside the rivers are used in making a mat covering for carports, arbours, terraces or, indeed, anywhere requiring protection from the hot sun. Basketwork is another local craft.

Travelling south on the old E50 there are two spas worthy of a visit, Curia and Luso. Both are top-class and very well patronised. It is strange to find such beneficial water in an area so rich in some of Portugal's best wine. If wine production is of interest, there is no better district in which to further your knowlege. A little south of Luso is the National Park at Buçaco. If you have not been to the Palace Hotel there, take the opportunity of having a meal or at least a cup of tea. A five-star hotel, it is one of the old timers of Portugal. Overly ornate and fussy in design, it is in a heavenly setting where the flora and fauna enthusiast can have a field day. Further south still is Coimbra, with one of the oldest universities in Europe. Its library is magnificent.

Below and opposite: *Moliceiros gather for a regatta at Murtosa.* MK

SANTO ANTÓNIO • SERÉM

THE POUSADA
Under young and enthusiastic management the standards have improved steadily. The swimming pool has been remodelled and a superb tennis court has been added in the grounds. This pousada was built in 1942 and was refurbished and decorated with taste in 1985. With excellent car parking facilities, and near the Oporto/ Lisbon and Aveiro-Guarda axis, it provides the ideal stopping place. The bedrooms are large and comfortably furnished. Although there is some traffic hum from the nearby roads, it is not obtrusive as the pousada is set high up in its own extensive grounds. These are well-tended by a management that is not only keen on gardening, but has an obvious interest in ornothology.

At the time of our last visit, the lady cook specialised, in good honest-to-goodness home cooking. Her Sopa da Vouga (the name comes from the local river, but there the similarity ends) is a first-rate vegetable soup. Pickled sardines, bacalhau, done something like the more common Bacalhau Dourado, fried quail, Vitela de Serém (veal) and roast suckling

pig from Mealhada are specialities, depending on the season. As the menu is limited, the food, freshly prepared and cooked, does justice to this well-run pousada.

We are now west of the Dão wine area and it is interesting to sample two or three of the wines available within a 25 kms radius. There are quite a few of them - both red and white. Any Borlido, Sogrape, Frei João or Solar das Francesas are recommended. In our opinion the 1968 Garrafeira of Solar das Francesas from nearby Anadia is one of the top six reds in Portugal - if you can come by a bottle. The '85 reds are ready for drinking and represent fantastic value.

From the reception desk to the restaurant, the staff are courteous and know what they are about. There are many little touches, from the old Portuguese prints to the modern watercolours, to indicate the care and thoroughness with which the pousada caters for its guests. It is possible you may wish to spend another night here. Getting to know a country is not all travelling.

Opposite: *The pousada.* E

HOW TO FIND
Fairly easy. The pousada is on high ground just off the main road from Coimbra to Oporto (10 kms north of Águeda). It is on the left-hand side of the road, shortly after crossing the bridge over the River Vouga.
Tel: **(034) 523230**
Fax: **(034) 523192** Telex: **37150**

FACILITIES

RECREATION

GRADE

SÃO JERÓNIMO • CARAMULO

THE AREA

Because of the climate, Caramulo was originally a sanatorium centre. Modern medicine has largely superseded its need. Of the 18 original establishments catering for victims of lung disease, 15 are now derelict. They had a brief respite as homes for immigrants returning from Portugal's former colonies. Now it is a perfect spot for a healthy holiday among the chestnut and mimosa trees that clothe the slopes near this well-manicured town.

The town has an interesting vintage car museum. A vintage 1938 Rolls Royce has carried two Popes, President Eisenhower and, in 1985, Queen Elizabeth II on her state visit to Portugal. Salazar's bullet-proof Mercedes Benz is also on show. For no apparent reason there is a miscellaneous collection of walking sticks which, in addition to their orthodox function, can also write, shoot, and provide a home for drink, snuff and sword. There is also a good art museum but the paintings of major artists like Picasso, Chagall and Dali are poor examples of their craft and do little to enhance their reputation.

Caramulo is in the Serra do Caramulo at a modest height of 750 metres, but the highest point is Caramulinho (1074 metres). From here, on a clear day, the view is magnificent with the mountains of Serra da Estrela away to the east. It is possible you have reached Caramulo via the pousada at Oliveira do Hospital. The road via Lagares, Ervedal, Oliveira do Conde, Beijos and Tondela (N 230), although not always signposted accurately, is a delight. Charming villages with humble picturesque cottages mingle happily with ancestral homes. The countryside is shaded by trees of many species, and Dão grapes grow in pockets along the way.

Tondela is the nearest town of any size, but surprisingly it does not have a tourist office although the local authority offices are most helpful. They explained the 17th-century fountain which is ornately decorated with typical Portugese 17th-century flair. Right at the top is a woman holding a trumpet. Why is she there ? Apparently because the sound of a trumpet played by a young lady used to warn the citizens of a possible attack by the Moors. "The sound of it" (*ao tom dela*), was corrupted to the Tondela we know today. It sounds plausible enough !

The region is interlaced with rivers. The ample water supply in these protected valleys encourages the growing of fruit and vegetables. The scenery is richer and greener than much of Beira Alta where rocky and barren wastes often merge with pine forests.

Below: A small Beira Alta town in the Arganil area. MK
Opposite top: Old Coimbra across the Mondego river. MK
Opposite bottom: Coimbra University's baroque library. MK

SÃO JERÓNIMO • CARAMULO

THE POUSADA
This creeper-clad pousada was opened in 1962. It is situated only some 50 metres from the steep road and inevitably there is the noise of traffic which is more noticeable at night.

Revisiting this pousada after a gap of only four years, it is hard to believe it is the same place. Last time it was difficult to find a good word to say. The food was indifferent; the wine list, which sounded exciting, was a figment of somebody's imagination as very few wines were available. The bedrooms had no baths - only showers. The whole place was insipid. The only real colour was in the swimming pool - a deep opaque green! Now things are very different and it is hard to get a room. All bathrooms now have baths as well as showers, and the swimming pool in its sylvan setting sparkles in the sunlight. The food is well prepared with daily changes of the set menu and a good à la carte choice. Bife à Pousada is prepared with cream, ham and pineapple, and was our choice. The wine list now reflects what is actually in stock and the Dãos, in either red or white, are a good accompaniment to your meal.

São Jerónimo is a useful staging post in the midst of some beautiful countryide. As it is so small, it is advisable to make reservations well in advance.

Below and opposite: *The pousada.* E. SR

HOW TO FIND
Fairly straightforward. Caramulo is on the road from Águeda (look on your map east from Aveiro on the coast) to Tondela (south of Viseu). The pousada is situated 1 km beyond the village of Caramulo, on the road to Tondela, on your left-hand side.
Tel: **(032) 861291**
Fax: **(032) 861640** Telex: **53512**

FACILITIES

RECREATION

GRADE

B

SANTA BÁRBARA • PÓVOA DAS QUARTAS

THE AREA
This is the true heart of Portugal. Even the nearby Mondego river, unlike many of Portugal's rivers, owes not one drop of its existence to Spain. Here in Beira Alta there is a great variety of scenery: forests; agricultural fields; vineyards producing Dão, probably Portugal's best-known wine; sheltered valleys with fruit trees; more open land with olive and cork; massive bolders in rocky outcrops; the pine-clad ranges sweeping up to the foothills of the Serra da Estrela. Elegant towns with spacious avenues, fountains and parks, jostle with humble hamlets. In a limited stay one is spoilt for choice and it is difficult to know what to include and what, unfortunately, must be left for another visit.

Some 13 kms to the west of the pousada is the town of Oliveira do Hospital. Outside the church, which has a good painted wooden ceiling, is a statue of a medieval knight. The town probably gets its name from the Hospitallers, a religious order of knighthood, who were the immensely wealthy rivals of the Knights Templar. Beginning as a hospital for pilgrims to Jerusalem during the Crusades, the order took on a more military role. The Hospitallers returned from Palestine with Henry of Burgundy, the father of Portugal's first king (Afonso Henriques 1139-1185). In more recent times they were known as the Knights Templar of Malta. The local museum is installed in the mansion of the local Cabral Metelo family.

A suggestion would be to travel north from Oliveira do Hospital on the EN 230-231 to the spa at Felgueira, passing en route some mature manor houses in very pleasant country. Then take the 234 to Mangualde to see the Palácio Anadia. If time permits have a peep at the ghostly and deserted Monastery at Maceira Dão. It is 5 kms to the west of the town and takes a bit of finding, but it is a rewarding digression. On again north to Penalva do Castelo where one's journey ends at the nearby Casa da Insua, a splendid 18th century mansion and one of the homes of the young and wealthy Duke of Albuquerque whose family ancestors developed Portuguese influence in India and Malaysia. This classic mansion dates from the late 1700s and is set in well-wooded grounds. Hopefully, it will soon be open to the public again as the grounds are now. A major burglary a few years ago necessitated its closure. Fortunately, most of the valuables have been recovered.

Local stone-built farm. MK

Top left: *Back street in Oliveira do Hospital.* SR
Top right and below:
Serra da Estrela, Portugal's highest mountain range. MK

SANTA BÁRBARA • PÓVOA DAS QUARTAS

THE POUSADA
This is a very well-run pousada under the direction of an experienced hotelier, Senhor João José Amaral, originally from the Pousada da Ria on the Ria de Aveiro.

Well-designed purpose-built, it was opened in 1971. There are several creative features: the palm tree-like supporting columns in local stone spring to mind. The general standard is that of a four-star hotel. It is spotlessly clean with modern but good furnishings. The bedrooms are spacious with verandas, and together with the principal reception rooms they look out on the lower slopes of Serra da Estrela.

Standards and amenities are constantly improving. Since our last visit a tennis court and an excellent swimming pool have been built. More and more pousadas have incorporated these amenities over the past few years. A little exercise after a day's travelling is good for body and soul.

Trout, Ensopado de Cabrito (casserole of kid) and Morcela Frita da Região(a fried blood pork sausage - not unlike the black pudding found in the north of England) are specialities. There is a table d'hôte and an à la carte menu with a good selection of sweets. Visitors with a penchant for ice cream will find those made on the premises mouth-watering.

There is plenty of car parking and the new east-west IP4 Guarda - Viseu - Aveiro trunk road makes this pousada a useful stopping place en route to Gouveia, Coimbra and Lisbon. 'IP', which puzzles many travellers, stands for *'Itinerário Principal'*. The construction of several of these main highways in recent years has opened up the country and greatly added to the speed of getting from A to B. It is, however, in the minor byways that the real Portugal offers her treasures.

HOW TO FIND
Needs care. Oliveira do Hospital lies about half-way between Coimbra and Guarda, just off the road, to the left. Ignore the signpost at the junction of the road leading into Oliveira do Hospital. Stay on the main road. After 4 kms you will come to the hamlet of Póvoa das Quartas. The pousada is in the hamlet, on the right.
Tel: **(038) 59551/3/652**
Fax: **(038) 59645** Telex: **53794**

FACILITIES

RECREATION

GRADE

Top and centre: *The pousada.* SR/E
Bottom left: *Deserted monastery at Maceira Dão.* SR

SÃO LOURENÇO • MANTEIGAS

THE AREA
Torre, one of the peaks not far from this pousada, rises to 2000 metres. It is the highest point of the Serra da Estrela, the highest mountain range in Portugal. The Serra da Estrela is as different from the plains and coastal pleasure resorts as the Pyrenees are from the south of France. Most winters, Torre gives the opportunity for skiing. Clube de Montanhismo in Covilhã or the tourist office can give further details. The area is at the centre of the National Park of Serra da Estrela - a beautifully eponymous name meaning Mountain of the Stars where walking through ever-changing scenery, from the cruel, imposing, upper slopes to the wonderfully wooded lower ones is good both for body and soul. Remember, at close to 2000 metres, the legs tire more quickly than at lower levels.

The local towns of Manteigas (originally famous for butter, as its name implies), Covilhã, Gouveia and Seia are places to be visited by car. Manteigas has a modern spa which was closed for improvement during 1991. As the map shows, the Serra da Estrela is laced with rivers and streams, the biggest being the Mondego. Keep an eye out for the water-wheels operating on the banks to irrigate the fields at a level higher than the water; later, dine on trout at the pousada's restaurant.

Poço do Inferno is a nearby waterfall, one of many in the Serra. In full flood, when the snows are melting, it crashes down the mountain with splendid force. Zêzere is supposed to be a perfect example of a glacial valley, but the rock formations at Cabeça do Urso (bear's head) and

Cabeça da Velha (old lady's head) might appeal more. In fact, staring at the shapes of these craggy pinnacles, the imagination can conjure up almost anything.

The road from Seia (N 231) climbs very steeply and the cross-country route, via Sabugeiro (which claims to be the highest village in Portugal) is not a good surface, but has all the atmosphere of this mountain range. At frequent intervals along the roadside are two-metre high posts in orange and black bands, a reminder to the fair-weather motorist that these markers may be the only indication in winter snow and fog of the whereabouts of this mountain pass. There is a lethal drop if you get it wrong. On these roads it does not take long to realise that the passenger has more opportunity of appreciating the view than the driver.

Ornothologists come from afar to study the bird-life and it is a great place for wildflowers. The wild pansy (*viola arvensis*) is one. Collect a few. It has a lovely name in Portuguese - *amor-perfeito* - "perfect love". There is an enormous difference between winter and summer climates - between the frightening grandeur of these freezing, sinister, misty peaks in January and the spring flowers and snow-capped friendliness of the mountains in the sunshine of May.

Top left: *Typical mountain waterfall.* MK
Top right: *Spring thaw in the Serra da Estrela.*
MK
Below: *Guarda cathedral.* MK

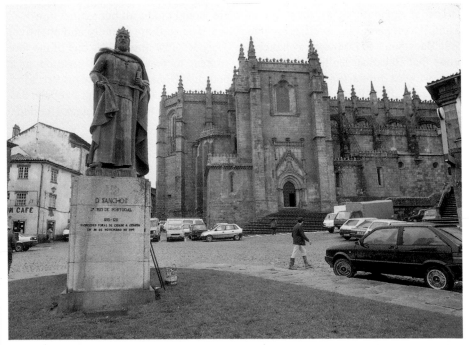

SÃO LOURENÇO • MANTEIGAS

THE POUSADA

This pousada experiences sub-zero temperatures in the winter, but has been built to withstand the elements. Outwardly rather forbidding, it was erected in local granite 45 years ago and, after modernisation, has been open as a pousada since 1980. The external appearance conceals the warmth of the welcome inside where there is good central heating, roaring log fires, double glazing with plaid blanket curtains and ample use of wood panelling. There is a general feeling of comfort and snugness against the worst the weather can occasionally offer. So popular has it become that this pousada has been twice extended and now provides double the original number of bedrooms.

The food is of a consistently high standard. It is difficult to single out particular specialities as they are all tastefully prepared and well presented. Give Bacalhau à S. Lourenço a chance to prove that Bacalhau Dourado is not the only way of preparing this typically Portuguese dish. Fresh grilled trout is always reliable. Follow it with Cabrito Assado à Serrana (roasted kid succulently

and tenderly prepared). Try and include the famous queijo da serra (a local sheep's milk cheese). Although Manteigas is on the fringe of the Dão wine area here is a good place to experiment with the local Castelo Rodrigo or the Covilhã Reserva. At one time there was an amusing idiosyncrasy when two half bottles cost ten escudos less than the full bottle! The water comes from mountain springs and is absolute nectar after a mountain hike.

Outside there is a terrace with breathtaking mountain views. You may see a Serra da Estrela dog, or at least a poor half-cast relation, guarding cattle. If you want to make sure of seeing this handsome mountain dog, António Lourenço breeds them on the northern slopes of the Serra outside Gouveia. Wolves have been reported roaming these upper reaches but are thought to be all but extinct now.

The staff are friendly and attentive. They are now directed by one of the few women to reach the top position in a pousada. Dona Maria José Craveiro, after experience at Caniçada and Palmela, has returned to her native Manteigas. Her smile of welcome rivals the scenery.

HOW TO FIND

Manteigas lies south-west of Guarda, south-east of Viseu and north of Covilhã. From Manteigas take the main road to Gouveia (38 km northwest) and travel for 13 km. The pousada is on the main road.
Tel: **(075) 981321**
Fax: **(075) 982453** Telex: **53992**

FACILITIES

RECREATION

GRADE

C Sup

Top left and centre: *The pousada.* E
Bottom left: *Bountiful mountain streams.* E
Bottom right: *Serra cheeses on sale in '*
Covilhã market. MK

MESTRE A. DOMINGUES • BATALHA

THE AREA

To enjoy this area with its great buildings and traditions it is desirable to have an idea, however sketchy, of Portuguese history. If you have visited the pousadas on the Minho you will know from the chapter on Dom Dinis at Vila Nova de Cerveira that on the 1st November 1386 a marriage was arranged between King João of Portugal and Philippa of Lancaster (Edward III's grandaughter and daughter of John of Gaunt). It was, in fact, part of a package deal. King João, then 30 years old, had the choice of two daughters - Catherine, aged 14, or Philippa, aged 26. Their father (John of Gaunt) promised, for his part, continuing support in João's fight against the Spanish. There was a slight complication in that João had taken an oath of chastity from the age of seven, but with papal dispensation they were married in Oporto on 14th February 1387.

In the same year, a defence and commercial agreement was signed by King João's ambassador at Windsor. The Treaty of Windsor, as it became known, has survived to this day and is the longest enduring treaty in history. Of course, the liason between Portugal and England had already been going on in an informal way for some considerable time with the mutual desire of defeating Spain. In August 1385, for example, with a small contingent of English archers, João had brilliantly defeated a Spanish force five times the size of his army at the Battle of Aljubarrota. This ensured independence from Spain for two hundred years. It was during this battle that the King vowed to erect an Abbey worthy of the occasion if he survived and won. Batalha (Battle) Abbey,

adjoining the pousada, is the result. In it lie João, Philippa and their four sons, one of whom was the great Henry the Navigator who was instrumental in Portugal's successes in opening up sea routes to Africa, India and America. The guidebooks give comprehensive details of the Abbey, a magnificent monument to an outstanding victory and to an outstanding family, but they do not all mention the unknown soldier's grave on which Queen Elizabeth II and Prince Philip laid a wreath during their state visit in 1957. The wreath is preserved in the adjoining military museum.

Twenty kms to the south is another architectural masterpiece, the Cistercian Abbey of Santa Maria at Alcobaça. Started in 1148 by D. Afonso Henrique, the first king of Portugal, it is older than Batalha. Both commemorate victory over invaders: Batalha, as we have seen, over the Spanish, and Alcobaça over the Moors at Santarém in 1147. Both have been extensively altered over the centuries, resulting in Manueline and Rennaissance architecture being married quite successfully with the original Gothic.

The aesthetic merits of one abbey over the other provide a source for endless discussion. Some people are persuaded that the scales are dipped in favour of Alcobaça. Not only has the building itself a magic; it has a spell over it. The story of King Pedro and his lover, Inês de Castro, who are buried here, must be one of the most passionate pieces of history ever recorded. After succeeding his father and exacting a horrible revenge on advisors who had murdered Inês, he had her body exhumed. He commanded that her corpse

Batalha Abbey. SR

be crowned and ordered his courtiers to kiss her long-lifeless hand. The King and Ines lie in facing tombs so that on Judgement Day they might awake to the sight of each other's eyes.

On the way to Alcobaça, try to find time to visit the battlefield where in the chapel of São Jorge, a pitcher of fresh water is always available for the traveller as a reminder of the thirst suffered by the troops on that scorching day in August 600 years ago.

Fátima (20 kms), the Lourdes of Portugal, has an enormous number of pilgrims wending their way to the modern basilica which stands on the site where three peasant children had a vision on 13th May 1917. They claimed the Virgin Mary appeared in an oak tree after a bright light in the sky. On the 13th October of the same year, a further apparition was witnessed - the last one to date. The commemoration on the 13th May and 13th October has to be seen to be believed. Up to a million pilgrims assemble in the great square and surrounding areas. The candlelit procession and singing create lasting memories. Pope John Paul II gave thanks to Our Lady of Fátima for his survival from an assassination attempt in Italy only to escape yet another attempt here.

MESTRE A. DOMINGUES • BATALHA

THE POUSADA
The pousada takes its name from the architect/builder commissioned by King João I to build the Abbey. In front of the pousada is a statue of Nuno Alvares Pereira (1360-1431), the king's general at the Battle of Aljubarrota. Previously a modern inn, the operation has been run as a pousada since January 1985. It is comfortable and well-appointed with one or two special touches showing thoughtful and creative design, like the under-lighting of the marble steps down to the bar. Try to get a bedroom overlooking the Abbey. There is also a pleasant suite.

You should have no cause to complain about the food but if you do, it will soon be put right. The staff were not offended when we returned the soup because it was not hot enough. There is an extensive à la carte in addition to the daily set menu. Specialities include Gambas com Natas (shrimps with cream), Bife Mestre Afonso (steak flambéd in brandy and mushrooms) and Açorda de Marisco (seafood and bread pap - which is much better than it sounds.)

The wine list is a good one. Your hostess, Dona Conceição, always manages to find some unusual and interesting wines like Vale de Fornos from the Ribatejo, or Terras de Demo from Trás-os-Montes. The Bairradas are also good value in either red or white.

If this pousada has a disadvantage, it is its closeness to busy roads and tourist gift shops. This is the price to be paid for being so close to an incomparable abbey, which has been a national monument since 1839. As such, it attracts thousands of people every year. It is a good idea to avoid August and the periods near the ceremonies at Fátima.

Pousada Mestre Domingues is a good place to learn a little history and appreciate architectural splendour in comfort. If the absorption of ecclesiastical architecture overloads the senses, the countryside around it is restful, being quietly devoted to the production of fruit and vegetables. It might also make a refreshing change to have a look at the grottoes at Santo António (10 kms)

Opposite top left: *Shrine of Fátima.* MK
Top right: *Fish is still racked and dried at Nazaré.* MK
Bottom: *Pousada with Batalha Abbey in the background.* SR

HOW TO FIND
Easy. Overlooking the famous Dominican Batalha Abbey.

Tel: **(044) 96260/1**
Fax: **(044) 96247** Telex: **42339**

FACILITIES	RECREATION	GRADE
		C

CASTELO • ÓBIDOS

THE AREA
The town of Óbidos is a national monument and has been carefully preserved. Some may find it a trifle 'pretty', but the cobbled streets, tiny travessas and white-washed cottages give it great appeal. From the moment of arrival at the main gateway to the walled town of Óbidos you will feel the welcoming atmosphere as you pass under its shady arches. This gateway is a gem with a gallery from which there is a glazed entrance to the small oratory chapel set in the walls and flanked by charming 18th century blue and white azulejos.

Despite its strongly fortified ramparts and castle that once commanded the open sea (the bay has long since silted up), the charm of Óbidos is somehow subtly feminine. Perhaps it is the profusion of flowers bordering the narrow streets, or the bougainvillea-clad walls, or the paintings of Josepha (1634 - 1684) in the church - or just an association of ideas. Since 1282 when King Dinis gave the town to his eight-year-old wife, Isabella of Aragon, who fell in love with it, Óbidos has been a great favourite with the ladies. Subsequent kings followed Dom Dinis'

example by making a gift of the town to their consorts. This practice continued up to the 1830's.

The castle, in which the pousada is located, was rebuilt by King Dinis on a Moorish site and it became a royal residence. Another young couple married here - Afonso V and his cousin bride, also an Isabella. Queen Leonor lived here, mourning the loss of her son and heir who was accidently killed in 1491 when returning from hunting. His body was brought ashore from the Tagus in a fisherman's net. The pillory in the church square includes her fisherman's net emblem as a sad reminder of this event. Pillories (*pelourinhos*) were not designed primarily for the punishment of criminals, as in many other parts. *Pelouro* means local authority. This one on the main street in front of the church square (Rua Direita) is a good example of a monument to the town's prosperity. The tourist office is in the same street and the museum is close by. The museum, funded by the Gulbenkian Foundation, has reminders that Wellington started his campaign against the French here in 1808.

Óbidos, which is within 100 kms of

*Left: **The fort, Berlenga Islands.** MK*
*Opposite page: **Óbidos viewed from outside and inside the town walls.** SR. MK*

CASTELO • ÓBIDOS

Lisbon, is only 7 kms from the sizeable spa town of Caldas da Rainha (Queens's spa). Legend has it that Queen Leonor, en route from Óbidos to Batalha, saw some people bathing by the wayside in some pretty foul-smelling water. They claimed the water possessed curative powers. They were so convincing that the Queen had a dip, was cured of her ills (unspecified) and donated her jewelry for the establishment of a hospital - the forerunner of today's Hospital Termal Rainha D. Leonor. Caldas has always been popular as a creative centre and many of Portugal's most famous writers, artists and potters were either born in the town or made their home here. Have a look at some of the work of the 19th-century master painter, José Malhoa, in the museum named after him in Carlos park. His portrait of Miss Laura Sauvinet is exquisite. Of the nearby seaside spots, S. Martinho do Porto is a safe natural harbour and supposed to be well-known for its blue shells. It took us half-an-hour to find one. There is quite a bit of residential development in this popular region and an enormous influx of foreign tourists which seems to increase year by year. You will hear every language but Portuguese ! It is best visited out of season.

Below: *Castle bedroom.* E
Opposite: *Fishing cove close to Peniche.* MK

Page 87 top: *The pousada.* SR
bottom: *Óbidos castle.* MK

CASTELO • ÓBIDOS

THE POUSADA
This early pousada, opened in 1951, is within the castle which has been much modified since Moorish times and survives mainly in the form of a 15th and 16th-century palace. The date on the keep is 1413. The popularity of Óbidos makes the nine bedrooms totally inadequate for the demand. Three of the bedrooms are in suites, each on two levels in the towers, which are especially popular with honeymooning couples. It is essential to make a booking well ahead and advisable to avoid the busiest summer months when the town is a seething mass. In calmer and more tranquil months it is a beauty spot which justifies its popularity. The construction of additional bedrooms would be a prudent expenditure.

The entrance, and a pair of adjoining windows to your left, are good examples of Manueline architecture. The accommodation lacks the grandeur associated with castles like Estremoz and Palmela, but what it lacks in size is compensated for by a friendly and informal intimacy. On the left of the reception vestibule is a small sitting-room and adjoining bar. The sitting-room sports a knight in shining armour - a little too shining to be authentic, but it sets the scene. There are some good pieces of furniture and tapestries here and on the first floor where the dining room is located.

The restaurant has an established reputation. Creme de Marisco, if you like fish soup, is well prepared. Bacalhau à Pousada is a typically Portuguese dish - not everyone's choice but worth trying once. Other fish dishes like shrimp cocktail, turbot and sole are all well presented. Frango na Púcara is a tasty chicken casserole and a speciality. So too is Cabrito Assado (roast kid). Lemon pudding is the best of the sweets.

The wine list is comprehensive for this is a good wine-growing area. It is worth trying a bottle of the reasonably priced local Gaeiras, in either white or red, or the Oiro d'Óbidos. The reds are gentler than some of the sturdier and darker wines common in Portugal. Have a bottle. Wellington didn't do badly on it ! Pay a visit to the nearby village of Gaeiras where the wine is produced and where there are a couple of good country houses to see.

HOW TO FIND
Very easy. In the small town itself.

CALDAS DA RAINHA
NAZARÉ
MATUREIRA
114
RIO MAIOR
115
Óbidos
S. GREGORIO
PENICHE
BOMBARRAL
LISBOA

Tel: (062)959105/46
Fax: (062)959148
Telex: 15540

FACILITIES

RECREATION

GRADE
CH

PALMELA • ESTREMADURA

THE AREA

A publicity leaflet from the reception desk describes Palmela as being five leagues to the south-east of Lisbon. If you are none the wiser, it may be more beneficial to know it is about 40 kilometres south of the Tagus bridge, just to the right of the connecting motorway (the turn-off is clearly marked). The magnificent Tagus bridge is now a bottle-neck at most times of the day and should be avoided during rush-hours and holidays. Originally named Salazar Bridge after the former dictator, it was renamed 25th April Bridge following the revolution in 1974. The Portuguese have a predilection for giving dates to roads, squares and monuments. Another six-lane Lisbon bridge is to be built further to the east, between Olivais and Montijo, and this could make the pousadas at Palmela and nearby Setúbal convenient bases from which to explore Lisbon, particularly if peace and quiet is sought after the city's roar. At present it is not practical and ENATUR are aware of the need for a pousada in the city itself. They already own a restaurant within the walls of the Castle of São Jorge, a marvellous vantage point for viewing Lisbon and the Tagus estuary.

The countryside skirting the motorway is flat and surprisingly sandy. It is only as Palmela is approached that the land rises steeply from sea-level. Palmela, founded in ancient times, probably got its name from the Latin word meaning palm leaf or victory. The views from the pousada are exceptional and enable the visitor, with the aid of a map, to get a very good idea of the lie of the land, and the sea for that matter.

Palmela is worth a stroll around. The market on Tuesdays and the wine festival in September are the highlights of the social calender. The adjoining Serra da Arrábida is a wonderful area for wild flowers. In the Spring walking over the hills is a journey of discovery. Within 5 kms of Palmela is the hamlet of Quinta do Anjo where excavations have revealed Neolithic burial grounds dating back 5000 years. The other road from Palmela leads to Marateca via Pinhal Novo and Rio Frio. You will be unlucky if you do not see storks either in flight or nesting on disused buildings. It is always a mystery how their precarious and exposed nests survive the winds which whistle off the sea in winter.

Below: *The pousada.* E

Opposite: *Lisbon's São Jorge castle at sunset and moonrise.* MK

PALMELA • ESTREMADURA

Find time on your way to or from Palmela to take the N 379 via Vila Fresca de Azeitão and have a look at the privately-owned Palácio and Quinta de Bacalhoa (15th century), and near Vila Nogueira the Quinta das Torres (16th century) and the Palácio of the Dukes of Aveiro (16th century). This was the area of the great country houses of the past. Now industrial development is on their doorstep. Factories, laboratories, bus depots and mills make uneasy neighbours with these grand buildings and gardens of the past. They are like ugly mongrels snapping at the fading robes of royalty.

In view of the closeness of the two pousadas, these notes should be read in conjunction with those on the pousada at Setúbal.

Below: *Dom Afonso Henriques.* MK

THE POUSADA
Nearly 250 metres above sea-level, this converted fortress occupies a commanding and virtually unassailable position. It was opened in 1979 and is a conversion of which the architect should feel proud. The approach is along a good tarmac road with one hairpin bend to the left which requires a couple of bites before it is rounded. Once up, there is plenty of secure car parking, and views which distract from the more prosaic task of booking in.

The origins of the Castle of Palmela are obscured by the mists of time, but we know it was taken from the Moors in the middle of the 12th century. In the 13th century it was the headquarters of the Portuguese Knights of St. James. After extensive damage in the earthquake of 1755, which also destroyed most of Lisbon, it was abandoned. The western boundary of the castle is occupied by the church and former monastery of St James, built by the knights during the 15th century: it is here that the pousada has been thoughtfully and successfully constructed. It incorporates the modern (there is a lift) while cleverly preserving the atmosphere of the ancient. The cloisters have been glassed in, as they have at dos Lóios at Évora, and provide a charming sitting-out space where drinks are readily served from the adjoining bar. The wisteria-clad courtyard is used in good weather as a further sitting-out area with plenty of sunshades. It is a pity there is no swimming pool. Sometimes in the summer months it would be more than welcome. There used to be one, but it collapsed and engineering problems in its reconstruction on the steeply sloping site

The pousada. SR/E

have not yet been overcome.

The dining-room seats 140 and has an adequate if not inspiring setting. The food is good. Income and inclination permitting, this is a restaurant in which to indulge oneself. It has won the National Gastronomical Cookery Contest with such dishes as Gaspacho da Pousada de Palmela, Arroz de Frutas do Mar na Cataplana (a delicious shellfish and rice concoction, cooked and served from what looks like a bed-warming pan) and Vitela Assada no Forno com Alecrim (roast veal with rosemary). On the set menu there are some imaginative specialities including Sapateira Recheada (stuffed crab), Sopa Rica do Mar (rich fish soup) and Linguado com Cerveja Preta (sole in brown ale). The menu is extensive and there are some 120 wines available. If you fancy a change from the better-known and local Maria da Fonseca school, try to get a bottle of Pedras Negras, a very drinkable full-blooded red from Palmela.

The bedrooms are spacious and well-equipped, but perhaps more suitably furnished for the summer than the winter. There is air-conditioning and most rooms

have the spectacular view already mentioned.

Over your pre or post prandial drink you might like to reflect on the castle's macabre background. Some say it is haunted. King João II (1481 - 95) was often called 'The Perfect Monarch' although it is doubtful whether the Duke of Bragança, the Duke of Viseu and the Bishop of Évora would have agreed. João II had the Duke of Bragança executed here in 1483. A year later the Duke of Viseu was stabbed to death in his bedroom. The Bishop was then condemned to the castle dungeons where he died within a week.

If thoughts of these medieval ghosts threaten to disturb your slumbers, fortify yourself with another glass of the local moscatel and remember that the pousada of Palmela has more recently hosted less notorious Heads of State, including President Mitterrand of France and the Queen of Denmark.

HOW TO FIND

Easy. If you find Palmela you cannot miss the pousada. Palmela lies just off the motorway from Setúbal to Lisbon, about 8 km from Setúbal.

Tel: **(01) 2351226/1395**
Fax: **(01) 2330440** Telex: **42290**

FACILITIES

RECREATION

GRADE

CH

Top: *Quinta of Bacalhoa near Azeitão has some of Portugal's oldest tile panels.* MK
Centre: **The pousada.** SR
Bottom left: **The pousada.** E

SÃO FILIPE • SETÚBAL

THE AREA

Setúbal is Portugal's fourth largest town and after Lisbon and Oporto is the third largest port. It is therefore a busy, industrial centre with the extensive Setenave shipyard a major employer of local labour. At the mouth of the River Sado, the town produces salt from the bordering marshes and is famous for its muscatel grapes, rice, oranges and fish from the estuary and open sea. Don't let the industrialised nature of the town put you off. There is much to see and much to interest the inquisitive.

The Church of Jesus is a must, if only to explain visually exactly what Manueline architecture is. Late Gothic, the rope-like columns are a reflection of the influence of the sea and Portugal's maritime supremacy at that time. The museum in the adjoining cloisters is interesting even if you are not especially fond of 16th-century religious paintings of which there are many. There is a nostalgic collection of memorabilia of Bocage, the Portuguese poet (1765 - 1805), and Luisa Tody (1754 - 1833), an internationally famous opera star in her time. There are streets or squares named after them as both were natives of the town.

Regular ferries cross the bay to the peninsula of Tróia which is believed to be the site of Cetobriga, a Roman and probably a Phoenician town from which Setúbal gets its name. Take your car if you wish to visit the Roman ruins (8 kms). Otherwise there is a passenger-only ferry. Tróia has been extensively developed as a tourist and conference complex. The 'rent-collecting boxes' which have been unimaginatively erected would do little to impress the Roman and Phoenician architects of the past !

The wonderful sea and landscape which surrounds this heavy industrial town is surprising. The Serra da Arrábida has been made a nature reserve and is a delight. It is quite a good idea to do a circular trip by car to the west of the town, perhaps going out on the RN 379 via Vila Fresca de Azeitão and Vila Nogueira de Azeitão and returning by the coast road via the popular beach of Portinho da Arrábida. The whole trip is no more than 100 kms and it will introduce you to the beauty of the region and perhaps prompt a desire to explore it

Below: *Thatched house in Sado Estuary.* MK

Opposite: *Serra da Arrábida's wild beauty.* MK

more leisurely. In Vila Fresca pay a visit to the privately owned Palace and Quinta of Bacalhoa, and in Vila Nogueira to the former residence of the Dukes of Aveiro. Nearby there is a splendid fountain at Aldeia Rica.

While you are in the region you may like to take in the countryside further to the west by continuing on the RN 379 which ends at Cape Espichel. This is often a windswept and barren spot which looks a little less forebidding on a gentle, calm summer's day. There are a couple of little chapels perched on the cliff edge which offer thanks to our Lady of the Cape (Nossa Senhora do Cabo), but give them a miss if you have no head for heights. Sesimbra is a little fishing town which, despite considerable development still has a charm and some good fish restaurants. Zambujal, which must be Moorish in origin, has some interesting caves. On the way there, if you have not overdone the palaces, go and see the Palácio do Calhariz.

As Setúbal is close to Palmela, where there is another pousada, the notes on the latter are equally applicable here.

THE POUSADA

The pousada of São Filipe is not for the infirm or faint-hearted. Forty well-worn steps lead from the car park to reception and there are more steps to the dining-room and bedrooms. There is no lift. Providence, rather than architectural design, has strategically located a little chapel two-thirds of the way up the route march from the car park. Here one may offer thanks for a mission so far safely accomplished and seek courage and determination to achieve the final destination sound in wind and limb.

The pousada was constructed over 25 years ago in a part of the 16th century St Philip's Castle which was built on the orders of Philip II of Spain (later Philip I of Portugal) who employed the Italian military architect, Filipo Terzi. The fortress was largely intended to thwart any possible attack from the English who had greatly damaged the King's reputation, self-confidence and prestige by the defeat of his Spanish Armada. The superb and commanding position gives views across the sea and the surrounding countryside of the Serra da Arrábida, a mountain range

Below: *The Pousada Tower terrace.* MK

Top left: *Serra da Arrábida.* MK
Centre: *Cove on the Arrábida peninsula.* E
Bottom: *The pousada.* E

SÃO FILIPE • SETÚBAL

protecting the bay of Setúbal and the mouth of the River Sado.

The government has learned much since this early conversion: the lay-out of the nearby Palmela pousada, for example, is infinitely more practical. São Filipe has a rambling lay-out on different levels. The bar is a considerable distance from the dining-room which is on another floor, and the two little reception rooms on the right of the entrance offer little in atmosphere. But what makes the place is the terrace. What a view! Here, under a sunshade, with a drink at hand and this 360° panorama around you, it would be surprising if the disadvantages did not evaporate.

In the first edition of this guide the food in the restaurant was given a justifiable slating, but there have been big improvements. Even oysters, for which Setúbal is famous, are now sometimes available in the season. Fish dishes have the edge over meat. There is a good wine list and the nearby Company of José Maria da Fonseca produces some very good and reliable wines. The firm has been in business since 1834, and their winery at

Azeitão is worth a visit if the subject interests you. Periquita, Pasmados, Camarate and Terras Altas in the reds, and BSE and João Pires in the whites are all thoroughly recommended. The last named is a little too sweet for some people's liking and it is more expensive. It is a good dessert wine , though, and leads on naturally to a taste of the famous Moscatel de Setúbal. Again, this may be rather sweet for your palate, but you should sip a chilled five-year-old on the terrace before a meal or a 25 year-old after dinner - it may change your opinion of sweet wines.

Before leaving, have a more detailed look at the *azulejos* (tiles) on the walls of the chapel visited on the way up. They represent various episodes in the life of St. Philip. They are by Policarpo de Oliveira Bernardes and dated 1736.

Although São Filipe is smaller and older than its neighbouring pousada at Palmela, many visitors, find Setúbal more friendly and more relaxing.

Opposite: *The pousada.* MK/E

HOW TO FIND

Easy. The pousada is in part of the ancient St. Philip's Castle. Approach via Av. Luisa Tody, the road which leads to Figueirinha.

Tel: **(065)523844/524981**
Fax: **(065)532538** Telex: **44655**

FACILITIES

RECREATION

GRADE

CH

SÃO PEDRO • CASTELO DO BODE • TOMAR

THE AREA

Tomar is a must, and the pousada provides a good base from which to explore both the town and the surrounding districts. Beside the river Nabão, it is an essential visit not to be rushed. The town owed its prosperity to the Knights Templar who drove out the Moors. Their order was dissolved by the Pope, but King Dinis (1279 - 1325) then founded the Order of Christ. Dominating the town is the huge Convent of Christ. Despite much damage by French troops in 1810, it is one of the wonders of Portugal - in the same division as Batalha, Alcobaça and Jerónimos. It incorporates many styles of architecture - Moorish, Byzantine, Manueline, Gothic and Renaissance, but they mingle agreeably. Prince Henry the Navigator became Grand Master of the Order of Christ and was responsible in the early 1400's for much of the present building. The wealth of the Order helped him plan the exploration of the oceans by caravels which carried the Cross of the Order on their sails.

There is a lot to see from the moment you enter the formal, box-hedged gardens of the Convent. A guided tour is helpful. One of the most striking parts is the Templar's rotunda, a 12th century model of the Sepulchre in Jerusalem. Octagonal-shaped, it is surrounded by a walkway with 16 sides. It is quite lovely. Notice the older, faded paintings on the stone arches, and the larger cross of the Order of the Templars as compared to that of the Order of Christ. An enormous, painted organ pipe was fortunately left undamaged by repeated French ransackings during the Napoleonic invasions. A second masterpiece is the central window which illustrates more readily than words what is meant by Manueline architecture. The cross of the Order of Christ surmounts the royal coat of arms. There is a mass of oak trees (whose wood served to build the caravels), rope-work, seaweed, coral, chains, globes and garters (from the English Order of the Garter). To some it is fussy and overpowering, but whatever your taste it is a masterpiece in stone by an unknown genius. You will never forget it.

Every third year in July, Tomar stages the Festa dos Tabuleiros, a festival of thanksgiving where the produce is distributed to the poor. The *tabuleiro* (tray) piled high with loaves, flowers, wheat and other produce must be as high as the person offering it. The trays are carried on the heads of the maidens of Tomar. Dressed in white, they are escorted by their menfolk in the procession. Meat is offered. Wine flows. Tomar is in fiesta and continuing a tradition of great antiquity.

If you wish to explore the lake and the islands adjoining the pousada there are rowing and motor boats for hire, and the larger, sightseeing 'São Cristóvão'. It is also a good idea to make the effort to travel south from the pousada to look at the much-photographed castle of Almourol in the river Tagus between Vila Nova da Barquinha and Constância.

Top left and right: *Tomar castle and its Renaissance Great Cloister.* MK
Below: *Castle of legends at Almourol in mid-Tagus.* MK

SÃO PEDRO • CASTELO DO BODE • TOMAR

THE POUSADA

The pousada is a conversion of the offices and auxiliary buildings of the engineers who constructed the dam between April 1946 and March 1952. The Barragem do Castelo de Bode is a damming of the river Zêzere and forms the largest artificial lake in Portugal. The tourist office, in the lee of the castle on Avenida Dr Candido Madureira, will provide a photocopy of the plans of the dam.

For somewhile, ENATUR (responsible for pousada construction) have realised that the location of São Pedro is not ideal. Unfortunately, the buildings are on the river side of the dam. They look out, not on the still, peaceful waters of the lake, but at a gigantic mass of concrete 115 metres high and 402 metres long. Efficacious it might be in helping to provide hydro-electric power and irrigation, but scenic it is not. It is a pity the pousada could not have been constructed in the buildings occupied by the Electricity Company of Portugal which are on higher ground on the lake side of the dam and command much better views.

The Secretary of State for Tourism instructed the architect José Santa-Rita to consider the possibilty of converting part of the Convento de Cristo, but the proposal has met with opposition and difficulties. Many consider such a development would be inappropriate within a building of this importance. The castle at Almourol would seem a far less contentious conversion.

Plans for a new site seem to have been delayed, but the Pousada São Pedro has undergone a major remodelling. It reopened in its newer and larger form in 1993.

The Adegas at Tomar and Almeirim produce some good local wines which are included on the wine list and may be purchased as half bottles. The use of fruit with some of the main courses shows imagination. Examples include Linguado Delícia (sole with bananas), Tornedo com Pessego flamejado (flambé filet steak with peach) and Pato assado com ananas (roast duck with pineapple). Chanfana (old goat stew) is a speciality. Like the goat water soup of the West Indies is a lot tastier than it sounds.

HOW TO FIND

Fairly easy. Tomar is the nearest major town. Look for the small town of Constância (30 kms south-east of Tomar). The pousada is where the Tomar-Constância road goes close to the barragem (lake) about 3 kms from Martinxel (a village off the main road).

Tel: **(049)381175/381159**
Fax: **(049)381176** Telex: **42392**

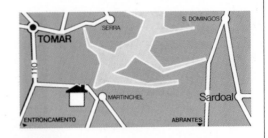

FACILITIES

RECREATION

C

Top left: *The pousada.* E
Centre: *View from the pousada.* SR
Bottom right: *Colourful national horse fair at Golegã.* MK

The Convento de Cristo will always bring people to Tomar, and nearby São Pedro is a busy pousada which over the years has deservedly gained a reputation for good food and courteous, friendly service.

SANTA MARIA • MARVÃO

THE AREA

Another fortress, Marvão looks down on the spa town of Castelo de Vide. At a height of nearly 900 metres, the air is fresher and cleaner than on the plains and there is the detached, independent feeling of a hill station. Castelo de Vide is a well-administered town with much to see. The helpful tourist office in the town centre will suggest a walk taking in most of the interesting spots. These observations, hopefully, will increase your enjoyment.

A charming legend explains how the town got its name (Castle of the Vine). The ravishing Guiomar loved Martim Gil. As luck would have it the husband Guimor's father had chosen for her died, but her father still wouldn't tolerate Martim and threatened all sorts of imprecations if she continued the affaire. The young lovers eloped to Martim Gil's castle where a large vine was growing. They called the place 'Terra de Vide' (Land of the Vine). The King requested the young couple to fortify, develop and defend the holding. As the town grew, the name was changed to Vila de Vide and subsequently, with the enlargement of the castle, it became Castelo de Vide. As if to authenticate the story, the vine forms part of the town's coat of arms.

The old part of the town and the former Jewish quarter are a delight. The 16th-century fountain there is a Renaissance gem and so too are the houses, alleyways and tiny squares. Have a look at the minute synagogue. Just down the Rua Porta Nova from the fountain is the spa. In addition to Castelo de Vide, a stay at this pousada provides the opportunity of looking at Portalegre, the district capital, and the much smaller Crato. A circular drive can take in both and give a good idea of the surrounding countryside. Go out on the EN 246 to Alpalhão; turn south on the EN 245 and Crato and the Flor da Rosa Monastery are only 15 kms. Prior Crato was literally 'King for a Day' in 1580 when the childless Henrique II died. His claim to the throne was convoluted, to say the least, and did not succeed. The impressive Monastery will be a future pousada - and a very fine one it will make.

Portalegre has a tourist office in Rua 19 de Junho. The architecture of the town is impressive, but you may find the local embroidery just as attractive. The workshops may be inspected and the petit point tapestries, many designed by famous artists, are good but expensive. They are worked in wool and have not the purity of design of the silk embroidery of Castelo Branco. The museum of Francisco Tavares Proença in the splendid Bishop's Palace of Castelo Branco is where the work is carried out. It is not too far north to visit from the pousada.

Opposite top: *The Marvão fortress.* MK
Bottom: *Castelo de Vide beneath the fortress.* SR

SANTA MARIA • MARVÃO

THE POUSADA

This fortified mountain stronghold is reminiscent of Óbidos, but on a smaller scale and not so commercialised. Close to the Spanish border, it has been a fortress since Roman times and many artefacts have been found nearby. The 13th-century walls and ramparts remain, but with some 17th-century modifications.

The pousada was converted from two private houses in 1976. It then had eight bedrooms, reception rooms and a dining-room. Its increasing popularity warranted an extension and although bedrooms were added a few years ago, the continuing demand for accommodation has justified a major redevelopment. The reconstructed pousada re-opened during 1992 with 28 bedrooms. One of the charms of the place is its excellent staff. Fortunately, during the building work they were employed at other pousadas - some at Santiago de Cacém's new Quinta da Ortiga.

The dining-room is a real 'roof-top rendezvous'. Splendid views and splendid food are an ideal combination. Add to this good wine and attentive service, and all the ingredients for a memorable hour or so

are at hand. It is always surprising to find the dining-room so busy. It is quite a climb to Marvão, but business people from nearby towns find it worthwhile and this, combined with visitors, makes it a much more flourishing restaurant than might be imagined. A pleasant hour can be spent in the adjoining bar studying the menu and picking out landmarks from your map - Serra da Estrela to the north (the highest range in Portugal), Serra de São Mamede to the south and west, and to the plains of neighbouring Spain to the east.

Despite the relative distance from the sea, the menu includes lobster, crayfish, prawns and turbot, often cooked with a coriander flavouring. Sarapatel de Cabrito is a goat meat soup which is not often found on other pousada menus. Partridge with a magnum of Periquita, followed by a good cheese is the keystone of a successful banquet. Two of the more expensive white wines are Catarina and Tapada de Chaves from the Portalegre area. Of the reds, Portalegre Reserva is a good buy and the non-vintage Alentejo wines are always excellent value.

The nearby convent of Nossa Senhora

HOW TO FIND

Easy. In the village of Marvão itself not far from the 13th-century fortress remains.

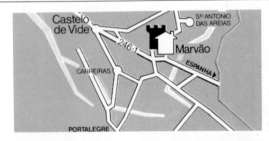

Tel: **(045) 93201/2**
Fax: **(045) 93440** Telex: **42360**

FACILITIES	RECREATION	GRADE
		C^{Sup}

Top left and below: *The pousada.* E. SR

da Estrela (Our Lady of the Star), founded in 1448, is supported, as the inscription says, by 'Love and Faith'. Ten sisters care for about 40 backward children and 20 geriatrics. The little chapel off the cloisters has a substantial weighing machine on which offerings of grain can be weighed. The convent is not officially open to the public but a donation to such a worthy cause can open many doors.

At the foot of this impregnable rocky battlement is some enjoyable countryside with groves of chestnut and walnut trees. The distances on the signposts are often marked 'approx', for time and distance are low priorities in these parts.

RAINHA SANTA ISABEL • ESTREMOZ

THE AREA

Still in the heartland of Alentejo, Estremoz is linked with the capital Évora (46 kms) by the RN 18 which sometimes prefers to be called the 802. It is an area steeped deep in history and produces some of Portugal's best marble. Earthenware pottery and carpets from Arraiolos are local products and so too are the wines of Alentejo which you can buy direct from the co-operatives in Vidigeira, Borba, Reguengos, Redondo and elsewhere. If these are too heavy or cumbersome to take home, an alternative is the locally-worked cork. Boxes in varying shapes and sizes are intricately carved from the bark of the cork oak tree (*sobreiro*) of which Alentejo has plenty. The barks are stripped every nine years. Farm workers often carry their lunches in cork 'tarros' and one of these makes an unusual and easily transported present.

There is a great deal to see around Estremoz and, as always, the problem is what to include in a relatively short visit. There is nothing of great interest on the road linking Évora and Estremoz except the over-restored castle on the hill at Évoramonte (18 kms). The stones have been so well cleaned that it now resembles a giant sand-castle. Try and visit a wine co-operative. The nearest is Borba (their Reserva is a very good red) and this leads on to Vila Viçosa which is more fully described in the chapter on the pousada at Elvas.

Our advice would be to tackle the area north-east of Estremoz. It is not so well-known and really gives the 'feeling' of Alentejo. To the north is the small spa of Cabeço de Vide. This can be approached by turning west at Monforte off the EN 18 to Portalegre, or east between Fronteira and Alter do Chão off the EN 245. Both secondary roads are perfectly adequate. A good idea is to go out via Monforte and make a circular trip by returning via Alter de Chão, Aviz, Fronteira and Sousel. Turn to the west in Sousel on the road marked 'Casa Branca 12 kms'. Turn left some 50 metres after this sign. This minor road, not marked on most maps, leads to the tiny chapel of Santa Maria which occupies a most commanding position with a spectacular 360° view. Next door is the isolated and oldest bullring in Portugal

The pousada. E

RAINHA SANTA ISABEL • ESTREMOZ

(and probably in the whole of the Iberian Peninsula). It is used only once a year - on Easter Monday at the Festival of Nossa Senhora do Carmo da Serra. For the rest of the year it stands empty. Sitting on the deserted terraces you can sense the atmosphere of the *tourada* ; stand in the ring and feel the hot breath of the charging bull and hear the cheering crowds. This is the real Alentejo.

Avis is the birthplace of the House of Avis whose kings ruled Portugal from the end of the 14th century to the end of the 16th century at the time of the country's greatest achievements. It is a fortified hillside town of considerable atmosphere and charm and yet not much visited. Alter do Chão is a town of Roman origin, once again with a castle, and the home of the national horse-breeding centre. It was origially a royal stud. The fountain in the central square is of elegant 16th-century design.

This part of Alentejo is also renowned for its metal work and some of the cow bells which you can buy in the bigger markets could be another reminder of your sojurn in Alentejo.

Previous page top: *Local shop.* MK
Previous page bottom: *National stables at Alter do Chão.* MK
Below: *Rug makers in Arraiolos.* MK

THE POUSADA

This sumptuous pousada is a conversion of the mainly 13th-century royal palace and castle standing within the walled town. As you traverse the drawbridge and pass under the gateway into the Largo das Portas, turn sharp right. From then on the pousada is clearly indicated. This is one of the most successful conversions carried out by the Ministry of Public Works and was opened by the President on the 26th September 1970. Much credit must go to the architects, Fernando Peres Guimarães and Rui Ãngelo do Conto. It was the home of King Dinis, who founded Coimbra University, and his wife Isabel who died here in 1336. King Pedro I also died here in 1367.

The royal residence suffered considerable damage when the powder room (not to be confused with the ladies' toilet) exploded on 17th August 1898. This is the date given in an official publication of the Ministry of Public Works, Buildings and Monuments. However, *Tesouros Artisticos de Portugal* published by Reader's Digest in 1982 gives the year as 1698. Both publications agree that King João V was responsible for considerable works of restoration. He reigned from 1706 to 1750 and it seems probable, therefore, that the earlier date of 1698 is correct. The oldest surviving parts are the Torre de Menagem and adjoining sections. The great tower, 27 metres high, is known as the Tower of the Three Crowns since its construction spanned the reign of Sancho II, Afonso III and King Dinis. Like the one at Beja, it is a landmark as one approaches the town.

The accommodation is well laid out.

Top left: *Marble is extensively quarried.* MK
Top right: *The pousada.* E
Below: *An ancient dolmen converted
to a chapel at Pavia.* MK

RAINHA SANTA ISABEL • ESTREMOZ

A spacious entrance foyer and reception area lead on to the drawing-room and bar. Also on this floor is the gigantic dining-room seating 200, with a fine vaulted ceiling. The well-furnished bedrooms can be reached by a staircase or the lift in the entrance hall.

The table in the dining-room is immaculate with spotless tablecloths and napkins, Vista Alegre china, and quality glassware and cutlery. The food is good as befits the setting. It is a restaurant which warrants a little extravagance on the part of the guest. Unless you are cheese-paring by nature or by necessity, it is a place in which to be extravagant and to give yourself a royal treat. Espadarte Fumado (smoked swordfish) is not unlike smoked salmon and makes an excellent starter. Another good one is Terrine de Cherne com Caviar (turbot terrine with caviar). Break away from the table d'hote and give the head waiter and chef a chance to show you what first-class Portuguese cuisine can offer. They will make recommendations for your consideration - possibly roast suckling pig, or medallions of venison, or wild boar, or partridge, or pheasant or something

plainer if you prefer it. Try to give them as much notice as you can to prepare and offer their very best. They love it, and you will have a meal fit for a king - indeed kings dined here. The head waiter will also suggest wines, very likely from the region, and the Borba Reserva, mentioned earlier, may well be one of them. Like the rest of the pousada, the dining room is furnished mostly with genuine 17th and 18th-century Portuguese furniture, tapestries, paintings and ornaments.

There is no need to venture far to absorb the atmosphere and history of Estremoz. Reading in your four-poster bed of Portugal's past, you will require no great imagination to see the tableau unfold.

Don't miss the little chapel, at the side of the pousada, which occupies the site of the bedroom in which Queen Isabel is presumed to have spent her last earthly days. Reception will tell you where to get the key and how to find the chapel for it is not well-publicised, but Capela da Rainha Santa Isabel must be visited. The Holy Queen was canonized in 1625, 289 years after her death, by Pope Urban VI. The blue tiled panels depict her life which she

---

HOW TO FIND

Easy. In the town itself, occupying a commanding position, it can be seen from the main road (on your left if you are travelling towards Badajoz and Spain).

Tel: **(068)22618/94**
Fax: **(068)23982** Telex: **43885**

FACILITIES

RECREATION

GRADE

CH

Top left and centre: *The pousada.* E. SR
Below: *The castle chapel.* SR

devoted to the poor. When challenged by King Dinis about her generosity to the needy, she opened the folds of her dress. The gold or bread (history is not sure which) concealed there had miraculously turned to roses. Opposite the chapel is a small but interesting museum and there are two other interesting churches in the square.

An excellent pool area and 11 more bedrooms have been added recently to this very popular pousada.

SANTA LUZIA • ELVAS

THE AREA

Elvas is only 18 kms from Badajoz in Spain (N 4) and to many travellers crossing the frontier this will be their first encounter with Portugal. To others it will be a return home to a country with familiar sounds and scents, and meals at more civilized times. Remember to check the time; there is often one hour's difference.

It is necessary to get deeper into Alentejo to appreciate its individuality and true personality. These frontier towns, which have seen so many upsets, are now prosperous and peaceful with little evidence of the xenophobia which characterised their past. They never seem whole-heartedly to belong to one country or the other. Their attitude is more pragmatic than patriotic. This does not detract from their very considerable interest, and following the frontier formed by the River Guadiana there are several fortified towns worthy of a visit. Alandroal, Terena and Monsaraz are three that commend themselves and are easily reached from the pousada.

Without doubt, the most impressive building in these parts is the Palace at Vila Viçosa. It is halfway between the pousadas at Estremoz and Elvas and can equally easily be visited from either.. It lies 5 kms south-east of Borba which in turn is just south of the main road about 13 kms from Elvas. To some, the Bragança Palace is a boring, uninspired monster. To others it is a powerful and dominating classic in which part of Portugal's history is enshrined. On approaching the palace square (Terreiro do Paço), the Knot Gate commands attention. The design is of entwined or knotted ropes and is typical Manueline.

'Manueline' gets its name from King Manuel (1495 - 1521) and, reflecting the maritime achievements of the country at that time, often included ropes, anchors and other nautical emblems. What makes it architecturally important is its originality.

The Palace, started in 1500, was built for the Dukes of Bragança as a hunting retreat. When finished in the 17th century, it became a favourite residence of the kings of Portugal (the House of Bragança ruled from 1640 to the end of the monarchy in 1910). Catherine of Bragança was born here in 1638. She married Charles II of England and English history would have been different if she had had children. Although he had none by his wife, Charles had many children from his various mistresses, including boys who became the Dukes of Monmouth, Southampton, Grafton, Richmond, and St. Albans (Nell Gwynn's boy).

There are guided tours around the Palace. Hitherto these have been conducted in Portuguese. Foreigners with no knowledge of Portuguese have found difficulty in following. Hopefully this problem will be overcome and the many foreign visitors will be able to get some idea of what is going on. We would recommend reading your guidebook beforehand.

For an amateur artist, the work of Carlos I is competent and appealing. The penultimate Bragança monarch, he spent his last day here with his son before they were both assassinated in the streets of Lisbon in 1908.

Opposite top: *Palace at Vila Viçosa.* MK.
Bottom: *Redondo folk art.* MK

SANTA LUZIA • ELVAS

THE POUSADA

The pousada occupies a busy position on the edge of the town. There has been a hostelry on this site for over 40 years. It was acquired by the government and opened as a pousada 22 years ago. It is a useful stop-over en route between Portugal and Spain and a good centre to explore this upper part of Alentejo, although many may prefer the more restful atmosphere of Estremoz or Évora. Elvas is a bustling, busy place with good shopping.

From the pousada you can see the gigantic Amoreira aqueduct, with 843 arches, designed by Francisco de Arruda who was responsible for the parish church in the town and for Lisbon's Belém Tower. The aqueduct was built on Roman foundations between 1498 and 1622. It took so long, as do many of today's projects, because of shortage of money. The fountain of São Lourenço was constructed soon after the aqueduct to receive the water in the town. The Largo de Santa Clara has a good carved pillory. Also in the town are good examples of wrought iron and the opportunity of seeing craftsmen working in copper.

We have never had a bad meal in the pousada's restaurant; some have been memorable. Specialities include Bacalhau Dourado (the dried codfish may look unappetising, but in the hands of a good cook it can be most tasty), Pézinhos de Coentrada (pig's trotters in coriander), Ensopado de Borrego (a special lamb stew), and Queixo de Porco na Brasa (pig's jaws) to mention a few of the slightly unusual dishes. They do a number of fish dishes, especially shellfish, very well indeed. Arroz de Mariscos (shellfish rice), Cataplana de Tamboril (monkfish), Pargo Assado (sea-bream), and Linguado Recheado com Gambas (sole with shrimps) are tempting. There is a good wine list, naturally and correctly favouring the local Alentejo vintages. Cericaia (a type of lemon soufflé), Capitolios, and the famous Elvas prunes are local sweets.

Elvas, a bustling town, has a fascinating atmosphere created partly by its ancient past and partly by its absorption of Spanish influences.

Opposite top: *The pousada.* E
Bottom: *The viaduct at Elvas.* SR

HOW TO FIND

Easy. In the old town which is reached by tuning left off the main road to Badajoz and Spain, going under the famous aqueduct and climbing the hill. Once there, everyone knows where the pousada is if you miss the sign.

Tel: **(068)622194/622128**
Fax: **(068)622127** Telex: **12469**

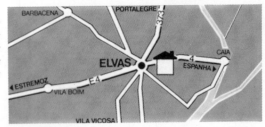

FACILITIES

RECREATION

GRADE

THE AREA

Alentejo is the largest of the Portuguese provinces and is well covered by its six pousadas. Largely a farming area with both cattle grazing and arable land, it is less spectacular than the mountainous regions to the north. It is not, however, a monotonous plateau like, for example, La Mancha in Spain. It is gently undulating country with here and there a ridge of higher ground. There are more trees than many people imagine and with improving irrigation there is a dusting of green over the landscape, even sometimes in high summer. The spring wildflowers are an unforgetable sight. Make no mistake though, Alentejo can be hot. Beja, 82 kms to the south of Évora, often records more than 40°C during July and August. It is the hottest place in Portugal. Unless you have an air-conditioned car, the Spring and Autumn are the best times to visit Alentejo. The interest in the region is in its history as well as its scenery. If old buildings and narrow streets are to be explored in comfort, the cooler weather makes it all the more enjoyable. A hot summer's day may sound very tempting when planning a holiday on

Prehistoric stones at Almendres. MK
Opposite: Alentejan fields. MK

a freezing winter's evening further north, but in reality a sweat-soaked shirt and dripping brow make the whereabouts of Vasco da Gama's house way, way down on the list of priorities.

There is much to see in and around Évora and a decision has to be made as to how much to take in before moving on to another pousada. Most people want to include the northern provinces during their holiday and this makes it impossible to visit as many places in Alentejo as you might like. Perhaps these brief observations will help to limit your choice, but certainly the more Alentejo is explored the more compulsive it becomes. It is a full day's job to do justice to the town of Évora itself but the central location of the pousada makes it possible without being too tiring. Outside the town there are numerous monasteries and convents, many now used for secular pursuits, but they all help to conjure up a picture of what this historic part of Portugal must have been like a few centuries ago. If saturation point has not been reached with historical buildings, have a look at some of them. Take the Alcáçovas road (RN 380). About 10 kms from Évora, before Tourega, is the village of Valverde where you will find the monastery of Bom Jesus founded by the cardinal King Henrique in the 16th century for the Capuchins. Now part of Évora University, this little building has an intimacy lacking in starker and larger monasteries like São Bento de Castris on the Arraiolos road. This may warrant a visit as it is claimed by many to be the first monastery ever to be erected in Portugal. It was founded in 1274. There are many others, but it would be a pity not to make time for a stroll

around Alcáçovas. Aim for Praça da República (on the right of the road as you travel from Évora). The Junta da Freguesia (Parish Council) has its office in the tiny square and could not be more helpful, although on our last visit the mayor was more interested in discussing the achievements of the local football team than details of the Ducal Palace. Fortunately, everything of interest is but a stroll from this square. The Paço dos Henriques is desperately in need of repair. 'Palace' is misleading - it is really a substantial town house facing the square but, of course, much has changed since its original construction under the orders of King Dinis. There is a very good *pastelaria* (cake shop) opposite and, duly fortified, the hundred yard stroll to the Barahona Palace is a cakewalk. This building is well preserved with impressive arched colonnades around its inner courtyard. It is sad the Paço dos Henriques is deteriorating by the hour.

On the other road, Arraiolos warrants a visit. An old town with a ruined castle, it is well-known as a carpet-making centre. The carpets are made by hand in a fairly loose cross-stitch weave and the designs are much influenced by Moors who occupied the country. You can see the ladies at work and may be tempted to buy. Arraiolos carpets, in fact, have proved an excellent investment. A 3m X 2m carpet which cost 41,400 escudos in 1983 would now fetch about 250,000 escudos. Perhaps an even better investment would be the petit point of Castelo Branco, but we must leave that for another day.

THE POUSADA
Opened in 1965, along with the one at Estremoz 46 kms further north, this pousada provides the most sumptuous accommodation in Alentejo. The Dos Lóios or St Eligius Monastery was consecrated to St John the Evangelist in 1491 and to this day the eagle emblem of St John has been retained. Just as the Lóios monks, in their sky-blue robes, dispensed hospitality and charity in the 15th century, so today on the same site this unique pousada offers the traveller the same warmth of welcome.

The cloisters have been glassed in to form a dining-room which retains its Manueline architecture and horseshoe arches, its vaulted ceiling and marble font. A meal in these surroundings, overlooking the central courtyard, is an experience which will remain in the memory. The menu is imaginative with several dishes which are not found every day. Alhada de Cação à regional is one. It is a garlic-flavoured shark steak and may tempt those not brought up on whale steaks in the '39-45 War. Cherne and linguado (brill and sole) are usually on the menu. Although expensive fish, they are well worth the extravagance. Suckling pig, pork and gaspacho, prepared in the individual 'Alentejana' style are good. So too are the game dishes in season. All pretty rich but there are some good local wines to go with them. Redondo, Vidigeira, Reguengos and Borba are all from Alentejo and it is not necessary to look further afield as they are available in both red and white.

The bedrooms are conversions from the original monastic cells. The furnishings throughout are in good taste and in keeping with this lovely building. There is a suite

Top left: *Pousada dining-room.* SR
Top right: *Temple of Diana under a full moon.* MK
Bottom: *Évora.* MK

LÓIOS • ÉVORA

with a luxurious baroque antechamber. If many of the Lisbon hotels with five stars warrant the accolade, this pousada, and the Rainha Santa Isabel at Estremoz, each deserve ten! It would be difficult to favour one above the other for they are both excellent, although the recently added swimming pool at Évora is something which Rainha Santa Isabel at Estremoz lacks at the moment. The pool may not be of Olympic proportions but it is very inviting after a day's drive or sightseeing and there is even a section for the children

On the doorstep are the well-preserved Roman remains of the Temple of Diana. The Temple was excavated in 1870, having previously been used as a slaughter-house. Portugal's 1974 bloodless revolution was planned beneath its Corinthian columns.

Évora, Alentejo's capital, warrants a leisurely exploration. It is a town of arches, arcades, aqueducts, azulejos, and academics. It had a flourishing university when, during the 15th and 16th centuries, the kings of Portugal made it the centre of court life. Manueline palaces, mansions and churches proliferated. Full of interest, Évora is to be savoured rather than gobbled.

It is outside the scope of this book to give a detailed account of what there is to see in the town - the local tourist office will provide a suggested itinerary and the better guidebooks devote several pages to the subject. If you have not the time or the inclination to devote many hours to exploration, certainly take a look at Praça do Giraldo with its arcaded but shady pavements, Casa Cordovil in Largo de Moura, the cathedral (next door to the pousada), and the older part of the city around Rua da Alcárcova de Cima. Also, if you have not seen the ossuary in Faro, the Chapel of Bones adjoining Évora's Church of São Francisco, constructed with the remains of 50,000 monks, offers a salutary reminder of our own mortality. So take it steadily. Stroll rather than hurry. You will find, with the aid of a dictionary, the streets of the "Countess's tailor", of the " Cardinal's nurses", of the "lisping man" and names of alleys as odd as the "unshaven man". Meander and muse; there is so much to see and admire - and it is all within a short walk of the lovely Pousada dos Lóios.

HOW TO FIND

Very easy. In the centre of the town facing the famous remains of the Temple of Diana.

Tel: **(066)24051/2**
Fax: **(066)27248**
Telex: **43288**

FACILITIES

RECREATION

GRADE

Top left, bottom left & right: *The pousada. E*
Centre: *The pousada in the shadow
of the Temple of Diana. SR*

VALE DO GAIO • ALCÁCER-DO-SAL

THE AREA

Vale do Gaio (Valley of the Jays) is in the heart of Alentejo. It is a peaceful area where the sounds of nature predominate. Salt-flats and paddy-fields fringe the River Sado which winds indirectly seawards; 'indirectly' because, like a dog, it seems to sniff its way along without any firmly preconceived idea of where it is going. It eventually reaches the sea at Setúbal where there is another commanding pousada. Before it reaches the Atlantic, the Sado passes through Alcácer-do-Sal, about 30 kms from the Vale do Gaio pousada by road (RN 5).

Alcácer-do-Sal is ancient. There are Neolithic remains in the museum there. The town gets its name (the castle of salt) from the Moors, and the ramparts look down on the Sado and the rest of the town as it stumbles irregularly down to river level. There are a number of cafes and restaurants along the waterfront where you can watch the world go by. A lot of north-south traffic passes over the bridge, so much so that a new one is being constructed. This is one of the main roads from Lisbon to Algarve. Once you are away from this artery, it is a different world.

Torrão, about 8 kms to the east of Vale do Gaio, is pleasant enough without being exceptional, and plays second fiddle as an agricultural centre to Alcácer-do-Sal. Make the effort to drive another 12 kms further north along the N 2 to Alcáçovas which has far more to offer. King Dinis, the farmer Monarch (1279-1325), liked the area and had a palace built so that he could spend more time there. Other noblemen followed suit and the palace of the Condes das Alcaçovas still has some 15th-century Gothic architecture remaining. The palace of Barahonas was another aristocrats' retreat. Near Viana do Alentejo is the imposing Santuário de Nossa Senhora de Aires. It resembles the Estrela Church in Lisbon and is typical of church architecture all over the world where Portuguese influence has made its presence felt.

This is a good area for game. If you are there for any time you should see partridge, wild duck and rabbit. Also, it is an area where it is difficult not to see storks, a protected species. The shepherds in Alentejo wear a 'Sherlock Holmes' type of cloak in the colder weather. Known locally as a *samarra*, it is made of sheep skin. It is sleeveless but has a sort of cape to protect the arms. It often has a wool collar, or sometimes rabbit or fox fur. The style may suit you !

Bullfighting has an authenticity here for this is the home of country folk and not of tourism. Remember, in Portugal the bull is not killed in the ring but merely wrestled to a standstill by the team of *forcados*. If you feel you would like to see a bullfight there is a good bullring on the eastern outskirts of Alcácer-do-Sal.

Opposite: *Sheep are reared on the Altenejan plains.* MK

VALE DO GAIO • ALCÁCER-DO-SAL

THE POUSADA
This small pousada is on the lakeside and has an intimate, welcoming atmosphere. Like the pousada further south at Santa Clara-a-Velha, it is a conversion and extension of the house for the chief engineer erected at the time of the construction of the Barragem do Trigo de Morais, more commonly known as Vale do Gaio. The damming of the River Sado and its tributaries was carried out in 1947-8 and the conversion into this attractive pousada was completed in 1977.

Peace is here in abundance. The gentle views across the lake from the terrace, the early morning viridian colouring particularly in the spring, and the rise of a fish breaking the still waters are all part of the scene. It may not be as spectacular as Santa Clara, but what it lacks in grandeur is more than compensated for by this private, secluded charm and a feeling that the whole scene was created especially for you.

This feeling is encouraged by a solicitous staff living on the premises who take a pride in their job. They will gladly tell you what they consider the best choices on the menu. They know the wines, although it is hard to persuade them that anywhere other than their beloved Alentejo produces good wine. On our last visit they recommended Esperão 1987. From Reguengos, it is not a cheap wine, but it is not well-known and is worthy of greater cognizance. It is first-rate with game, which is available in season. For such a tiny pousada the food in enterprising and well-prepared. Perhaps the standard pork dishes, for which the Alentejo is famed, are the best, but Senhor António de Freitas, the director, ensures that everything on offer is good. The bedrooms are adequate but have no baths, only showers.

This is excellent walking country and a paradise for dogs. Fir trees are tapped for their resin. There are cork oaks, eucalyptus, and acres of paddy-fields which were originally salt-flats fringing the river. The water attracts bird-life and a pair of binoculars is useful for seeing the smaller species. Mosquitoes, unfortunately, are also attracted. This was formerly a malarial area but, of course, malaria has long since been eradicated. If you are prone to insect bites, an anti-mosquito cream or spray is a

HOW TO FIND

Not easy. Take the Beja road out of Alcácer do Sal. After about 27 km - about 8 km from Torrão - a semi-paved road on the right (marked "Pousada") takes off at a right angle. Drive on through the woods for about 4 km.

Tel: **(065) 669610**
Fax: **(065) 669610** Telex: **15118**

FACILITIES	RECREATION	GRADE

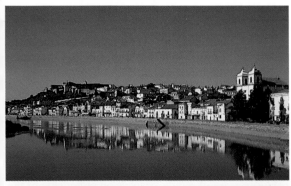

Top left: *Alcáçer do Sal.* MK
Centre: *The pousada.* SR
Bottom right: *Typical stork nesting site.* E

useful safeguard during the hot, still months of summer. Fishing, swimming in the lake (there is no pool) and rough shooting are all available.

Vale de Gaio is a joy at any time of the year. For many, the winter is a favourite. After the searing heat of the summer is over, walking is a pleasure and not an effort. A roaring log fire in the chill of the evening is difficult to leave. If you want to 'get away from it all', the Valley of the Jays is the place.

SÃO TIAGO • SANTIAGO DO CACÉM

THE AREA
The road north from the Pousada at Sagres follows the western seaboard of Portugal. After Aljezur and Odemira, the RN 120 reaches Santiago de Cacém en route to Lisbon. This used to be the main road from Algarve to the capital until the new and faster north-south road was constructed further to the east. But our aim is not speed, it is to enjoy and explore the countryside. From the time the barren landscape of the Sagres peninsula is left behind at Vila do Bispo, the scenery improves. Eucalyptus trees line the route; a pine forest comes into view; the land is cultivated and productively green. On the high ground a windmill dominates the skyline and a donkey plods homewards with a load which would intimidate most forms of mechanised transport.

Along this west coast are many magnificent beaches, not so well-known as the southern Algarvian beaches but, nonetheless, among the best in Europe. They are popular with the Portuguese and being nearer Lisbon are fairly crowded in summer, particularly in the month of August. There are so many of them, and they are so vast, that a quiet spot is not difficult to find. Take care, however, to observe elementary swimming precautions. Do not swim on an outgoing tide or when it is rough, and observe the flags and lifeguards' instructions.

Near the pousada, there are two inland lagoons at Santo André where you can relax and enjoy a good eel stew. Further south and on the other side of Sines, Porto Covo must be put on your itinerary. Not far off-shore is the fortress island of Pessegueiro with its air of mystery

and intrigue. The locals fish off the rocks using rafts which look as though they were the forerunners of Kon-Tiki.

Further south, but still within easy reach, is the equally attractive Vila Nova de Milfontes. The village is at the mouth of the River Mira which flows from the Santa Clara resevoir where there is another pousada overlooking the dam. There are good, sandy beaches on either side of the river's mouth and the ivy-clad castle discreetly takes in paying guests. Odemira and Ourique are pleasant small towns but not worth a special visit.

Since 1971, Sines (17 kms) has become an increasingly commercialised port. It is a major tanker-terminal. Surrounding the town, the birthplace of Vasco da Gama, huge refineries house the country's strategic oil reserves. This necessary development has done little to increase the touristic appeal of the town, but it has improved the road network.

Sines, Vasco da Gama's birthplace. MK

Top left: *Mira river winds its way to Vila Nova de Milfontes.* MK
Top right: *Fishing harbour at Sines.* MK
Bottom: *Porto Covo.* E

SÃO TIAGO • SANTIAGO DO CACÉM

THE POUSADA

The pousada, which opened in 1947, is nowadays far less a staging post en route to Lisbon than a tourist centre from which to explore the west coast. Situated on the outskirts of the town, this creeper-clad pousada resembles a small country house. The grounds are well-wooded and screen the nearby main road and traffic noise.

Considerable work has recently been undertaken to modernise the bedrooms both in the main house and the annex. The swimming pool has been overhauled and is most welcome, as is the shaded and wisteria-clad terrace adjoining. Senhor Aníbal de Brito, originally from the pousada at Aveiro, directs operations with experienced skill.

The menu is restricted, but constantly changing which ensures that the food offered is specially prepared. Perna de Porco Molho Maçã (leg of pork with apple sauce) and Linguado à Moda da Casa (sole) are really very well done - so too are the soups such as gaspacho and Açorda Alentejana. There is a good and interesting selection of wines. Colares from the Ramisco vine, the only one to escape the deadly phylloxera of the 1870s and 1880s, is considered by many to be Portugal's best. Palmelas, Dãos and vinho verdes are in stock. The black and white uniforms of the staff are smart and the service is attentive and professional. The dining-room opens on to the spacious terrace where coffee and liquers or an aperitif go down well.

Before moving on, have a look at the castle and church which dominate the town. The Knights Templar were responsible for its construction and it gives a good viewing point over the town, the pousada and surrounding countryside. Also within walking distance of the pousada (1.5 kms) are the Roman ruins of Mirobriga.

One of the snags with the Pousada de São Tiago was the difficulty of getting a room. It always seemed to be full. Extensive modernization has taken place and the accommodation now offered is excellent. To relieve the congestion, ENATUR had the foresight to purchase the nearby Quinta da Ortiga and turn that into a pousada as well. For details, turn to pousada number 31 on page 148.

HOW TO FIND

Fairly easy. Santiago de Cacém, lies 17 kms from Sines (on the coast) at the junction of the roads from Grandola (north) and Beja (east). The pousada is on the outskirts of the town, on the road from Grandola, on the left, opposite a garage/filling station.

Tel: **(069)22459**
Fax: **(069)22459** Telex: **16166**

FACILITIES

RECREATION

GRADE

B

Top left and bottom: *The pousada.* E
Below: *Sunset over Vila Nova de
Milfontes.* MK

SÃO GENS • SERPA

THE AREA

Serpa is a very good base for exploring the lower eastern side of Portugal and a good staging post when entering or leaving Portugal (the frontier is 30 kms to the east along the fast RN 260). Travelling in the other direction, the RN 260 brings Beja (again about 30 kms) within a short drive. If you wish to continue to the smaller pousada on the lake at Vale do Gaio, take the equally good RN 121 from Beja to Ferreira - it is clearly indicated; turn north there to Torrão (N 2); Vale do Gaio is about 8 kms on the Alcácer do Sal road (N 5). All around is extensive farming land with vast fields of grain, and around Serpa vines, cork oak and olive trees thrive.

Travelling south is interesting. Aim for Mértola an ancient town on the banks of the Guadiana. It has a distinctly Moorish atmosphere - some of the notices are in Arabic - and the church is a conversion from an original mosque. You can see the Moorish mihrab behind the present altar where, facing Mecca, the faithful were summoned to prayer. On the way you will pass Sandomingo whose church tower is surmounted by a clock. At first it seems strange to see the maker's name - Bennet, 65 Cheapside; only on enquiry does it become clear. Sandomingo was a copper mine which shut down about 30 years ago. It was British financed and employed some 7000 people. The clock (if not the church) were probably also financed from Britain. There is nothing in the church of interest, but the lake adjoining the road is a good spot for a picnic.

Further south on the RN 122 you enter Algarve. A signposted turnoff takes you to the remote village of Alcoutim. Again, this is on the river Guadiana with a fort overlooking its Spanish counterpart on the opposite bank. Time is not a priority in these parts. It is lonely and isolated, but the journey is not unpleasant and the Cafe O Soeiro, on the water's edge by the church, does a good barbecued chicken. Local boatmen will arrange a run up or down stream. A longer and very enjoyable river trip is from Vila Real de Santo António. This can be arranged through the tourist office there. If you are then thinking of a stop at the pousada at São Brás, the countryside en route is among the least inhabited in Algarve. The whole area gives a pioneering lift to the spirit.

Olive trees. MK

Top left, right and bottom right: *Olive trees and solitary farms dot the great spaces of the Alentejo.* MK
Centre: *Mértola's church, originally a Mosque.* MK

SÃO GENS • SERPA

THE POUSADA
Built 25 years ago, the pousada stands on high and commanding ground with immense views across the plains of Alentejo and to the Sierra de Andevalo in Spain. Money has been spent on improvements and a swimming pool has been added to refresh tired limbs after a day's travelling. Although modern, the bedrooms are spacious with balconies offering fantastic views. There is also a fine terrace adjoining the dining-room and lounge.

The food is standard Alentejo cuisine with pork as the main meat, cooked in a variety of ways. In addition to the set menu there is an À la carte with six hors-d'oeuvres, and four dishes each of fish and meat. Of the meat dishes, the Ganso de Vitela Estufada com Congumelos (veal stew with mushrooms) is a great favourite. It is not difficult to find a good wine to wash it down. Anything from Borba, Redondo, Reguengos or Vidigueira either in red or white, is very reliable. It is a pity that the even more local vinho de Pias (14 kms) is missing from the list. Cheese from Serpa is good and has now been included. It is of the Serra family, made from ewe's milk and is a welcome addition to the cheese board. Perhaps the Pias will be available next time. Meanwhile, to accompany the cheese why not Quinta de Carmo from Estremoz? Or you might care to try a glass of Madeira - there is one rejoicing in the name of Rainwater Medium dry. It must be good to survive such a nomenclature.

The town itself has seen more prosperous days commercially. The copper mine at Mina de Sandomingo used to bring quite a lot of business to Mértola and Serpa. The commercial loss has, in fact, been the tourist's gain. The streets are narrow and picturesque with plenty of ironwork protecting first-floor balconies. There are squares, both small and large, with an atmosphere of tranquility. Serpa is a place to explore on foot. Have a look at the mellowed aqueduct, the church, the 14th-century clock tower, and the castle destroyed and rebuilt so many times in the turbulent past of this walled city. Craftsmen work in wood, cork and horn, making drinking vessels, spoons and ornaments.

HOW TO FIND
Fairly easy. Take the road out of Serpa and travel towards the frontier with Spain. After about 3 kms you will see the pousada on your right, standing on a hill, up a small track.

Tel: (084)53724/5
Fax: (084)53337
Telex: 43651

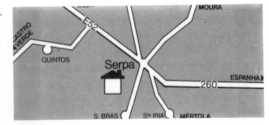

FACILITIES

RECREATION

GRADE
C

Top right: *Mértola castle was originally Roman.* MK
Below: *The pousada.* SR

The local singing and music group Os Ceifeiros de Serpa epitomises the happy atmosphere of this enchanting little town. Don't rush to leave Serpa. The longer you stay the more you will find: windows, doorways, fountains, chimneys, watermills, wells, all reflecting the influence of Romans and Moors whose home this was. You will pack your bags with reluctance. Before you do, have a peep at the tiny chapel adjoining the car park of the pousada. Capela de Nossa Senhora de Guadalupe (sometimes called Capela do Altinho) is probably 14th century, although the custodian claims it to be 9th century. It has more letters in its name than it has seats, and it is one of the few churches with a survey beacon in its structure.

SANTA CLARA • SANTA CLARA-A-VELHA

THE AREA

The pousada is about three hours drive south of Lisbon. The journey is largely through flat farming country - the granary of Portugal - and the huge artificial lake of Santa Clara provides much needed water to the lower Alentejo. Travelling south, the road very shortly commences to climb the Serra de Monchique, a mountain range which forms the boundary with Algarve. This road to Monchique (33 kms) provides some marvellous mountain scenery, perhaps better enjoyed by the passengers than the driver who has to concentrate on negotiating the twists and turns. On either side of the road the land sweeps away in great ranges of fir, eucalyptus and cork. The bark is stripped from the cork trees every nine years. Nave Redonda, which is passed en route, is a big cork-collecting centre. The surface of the road could be better, but since the journey is not one to be done in a hurry it does not really matter. It gives a chance to observe things which can so easily be missed if speed takes precedence. You may be lucky enough to see a mongoose and there are plenty of partridge about in this sparsely populated mountain range.

Monchique, when you reach it, is a mountain village which has moved into the 20th century with reluctance. The views to the coast are exceptional. Unfortunately, visibility is impaired quite often by a heat haze. Fóia (902 metres) is the highest point in the range. On the road from Monchique to Fóia there are half a dozen restaurants specialising in the local dishes of piri-piri chicken (charcoal grilled with a chilli sauce) and *presunto* (smoked ham). Washed down with a glass of red these need some beating. Explore Monchique on foot; some of the most interesting sights are to be found in little tiny alley-ways where you come across a barber, a blacksmith, a woman cooking sardines on a little fire on her doorstep, and a minute shop which has not quite made up its mind whether it is a bar or mini-market.

Further south is Caldas de Monchique. There has been a spa here since Roman times. Some believe that the great Hannibal landed on the coast and watered his elephants at Caldas prior to climbing the Serra de Monchique - a sort of dummy run for his eventual Alpine crossing. It is an oasis to the right of the Monchique-Portimão road. The village square is fringed by a Moorish-looking spa building where you can sip the bicarbonated waters. The Portuguese King, João II, claimed the waters cured his illness in 1495. They could not have been all that efficacious as he died the same year. Today, it is a well-attended health resort with a good record of success in dealing with rheumatic complaints

Ripening gourds. MK

Top left: *The village of Santa Clara.* MK
Top right: *Serra de Monchique.* SR
Centre: *Alentejo beaches are usually dazzling - deserted.* MK
Bottom right: *Arbutus berries used in the making of a local aguardiente called Medronho.* E

THE POUSADA

This tiny pousada was opened in 1971. The building was originally the office and home of the chief engineer in charge of the construction of the Barragem de Santa Clara. A vast artificial lake formed by damming the River Mira and its tributaries, it now gives much-needed water to surrounding farmlands. Today the former office site provides the perfect position to overlook the sheltered waters which are 44 kms long and up to 90 metres deep. It is a wonderfully peaceful and tranquil scene with the waters enclosed by slopes of fir and eucalyptus. Sailing, swimming, fishing, walking and duck shooting are available sports - the first four without formality although a licence from Odemira is required for shooting.

The cuisine is good and personal. Gaspacho a Alentejana and Sopa Alentejana (an intriguing, if slightly mysterious soup with a poached egg lurking in its midst) are specialities. So too is Ensopado de Cabrito (stewed kid). Alentejo is also famed for its pork and the pousada's chef prepares it very well. The table wine Casal do Castelão is a good accompaniment. Romeira is another red which is at home with most of the dishes. From time to time there are little and endearing personal touches at the table such as a rose for each lady guest.

There is a minute swimming pool in gardens which improve each year. Swimming in the lake is a more adventurous and less restricting alternative. The water, considering its depth, is surprisingly warm in the summer.

Sipping a drink on the terrace and absorbing the beauty and peace makes sightseeing something to do tomorrow. Nevertheless, the nearby agricultural village of Santa Clara-a-Velha is pleasant to stroll around. Many of the street names (India, Goa, Dom Henriques) remind the traveller of Portugal's great past and of her former overseas possessions. Restaurant Pancada serves *Achegã* freshly caught in the *barragem*. Interestingly, the word does not appear in any of the Portuguese dictionaries. It is probably a corruption from 'Michigan', where a Portuguese working on the lake saw a similar fish. It is a bony, freshwater fish of the bass/perch family, quite tasty if well-prepared and

HOW TO FIND

Needs care. 21 kms from Odemira on the Ourique road you come to Odemira railway station and the juction of the road going south to Santa Clara-a-Velha. Go past the town and take the first proper road on your left; this leads, after 4 kms, to the pousada.

Tel: **(083)98250**
Fax: **(083)98402** Telex: **56231**

FACILITIES

RECREATION

GRADE

Left: *The pousada.* E
Below: *View from the pousada.* E

cooked - but watch out for the bones. There are proposals to introduce other fish and certainly a few juicy trout would be welcome.

The summer attracts a lot of campers. Instead of being confined to a particular area they are allowed to spread themselves around the lake shore. This does not enhance the scenery.

If you are a rowing enthusiast you may see the Eton boat practising on these wonderfully secluded and peaceful waters during the school's summer holiday.

On our last visit the pousada looked seedy with worn carpets and decorations which needed attention. The explanation was that it was shutting for a major face-lift and modernisation. The reopening was said to be scheduled for July 1993. Check in advance if it is open because there is little alternative accommodation in the vicinity.

SÃO BRÁS • S. BRÁS DE ALPORTEL

THE AREA
Algarve, the best-known holiday region in Portugal, is famous for its sandy beaches, its lush golf courses and its international hotels. Without detracting from these superb facilities, there is much more to Algarve than the razzamatazz of get-brown-quick package tourism. It is a region of contrasts, from coastal plains to magnificent mountain scenery, from the parched lowlands to the fast flowing streams of the hinterland. It is a region of quaint chimneys and traditional crafts and customs, of almond blossom and eucalyptus trees, of mimosa and cork oaks, of palms and firs and kind, gentle people who, even if they do not understand what you are saying, convey by a look or a smile a welcoming friendship.

Faro, the capital of Algarve, has an international airport which is about a 35 minute drive from the pousada. The town has a good shopping centre with many roads confined to pedestrians. The guidebooks tell you what to see in Faro, but may overlook a couple of unusual features. The chapel of the bones, alongside the cathedral, is one of several throughout Portugal and Spain, but this chapel is a macabre gem of construction. Made entirely of the skeletons of exhumed monks, it reminds us that 'These bones are waiting for yours'. Out into the sunlight again and not far distant is the enchanting Teatro Lethes. A true Thespian jewel, this little theatre, originally a chapel, was erected by an Italian family who made money in the region after being shipwrecked on their way to England. We owe a vote of thanks to Dr. Lazaro Doglioni for it was his enthusiasm in the 1800s which created this mini La Scala. If you are in Algarve during the months when the annual Algarve Music Festival is held, you may be lucky enough to see a performance at the Teatro Lethes. Details of the programme, usually from the end of April to the end of June, can be obtained from the local tourist office.

A number of well-converted and modernised private houses are situated in the vicinity, some of the most attractive being in the Bordeira area. It is encouraging to see these lovely old buildings being restored and not pulled down to make way for the sort of uninspired architecture which has become only too common in Algarve.

Estoi, 8 kms south, has a palace which cries out for similar loving restoration. Not far from the church a magnificent avenue of palms leads past an old stable block to the Palácio de Estoi, once the home of the Counts of Carvalhal. 'Palace' is euphuistic. It is really a moderately-sized country house. Unoccupied, this 18th-century relic, desperately needs attention. The still fountains need the laughter and animation of cascading water. The bandstand needs musicians and mirth. Sadly, all has been silent for years but money has now been allocated for restoration work. The nearby Roman ruins of Milreu are a disappointment too, many of the objects unearthed having been removed to museums.

Loulé (13 kms on N270) is a sizeable and expanding market town. Its tree-lined main avenue resembles a minor Avenida da Liberdade in Lisbon. The place has a distinctly Moorish atmosphere which is apparent in the Market building.

Although the construction is relatively modern it recalls Cordoba or the Alcazar in Seville. The fruit and vegetables somehow always taste better from Loulé market.

If you take the road north from the pousada via Alportel, just south of Barranco do Velho the N124 to your left runs more or less parallel with the much more frequented coast road. It passes through Alte (worth a stop to see the fountain and grottoes), S. Bartolomeu de Messines, and on to Silves, the original capital of Algarve. Just before Silves, to the right of the road, is a reservoir which provides a charming lakeside setting. Silves has a castle with some pleasant, shady gardens and ramparts overlooking the river Arade. From Silves the road north leads through the mountains to the village of Monchique from where, on a clear day, the view of the whole of the Algarvian coastline is a sight to remember.

SÃO BRÁS • S. BRÁS DE ALPORTEL

THE POUSADA

Apart from the pousada on the coast at Sagres, this is the only other one in Algarve and it is well-placed to explore the eastern coastal resorts and to play golf at the excellent courses of Vale do Lobo, Quinta de Lago and Vilamoura.

This pousada was one of two original purpose-built government projects in 1942. It received a major face-lift in 1975 and has been further improved since. Quite recently a very fine swimming pool and an all-weather tennis court were installed to add further to guests' comfort. Filomena, who has been a receptionist here for thirteen years, can usually find you a racket and balls if you have not brought them.

On the culinary front there is Espetada de Gambas À Pousada which is charmingly translated as Prawns on Spike. The stewed lamb and a number of fish dishes cooked in a *cataplana* (a copper mussel-shaped pot) are excellent. So too is the Arroz de Mariscos (a rice and shellfish concoction).

Page 141 top left: *Typical Algarve cottage.* MK
Top right: *Children delight in carnival.* MK
Centre: *Fisherman's beach, Albufeira.* MK

Your hosts are Senhor Pedro Leite, who is from Lisbon, and his wife Luisa, from Chaves. They are never far from the centre of activities and are justifiably proud both of their origins and their pousada. The local wines from the Co-operative at Lagoa, with their 13% alcohol content, are too strong for many people, particularly in the heat of the Algarvian summer. You may be happier with a white. If so, try Planalto. This is produced by the reliable Sogrape Company. It comes from the Douro region and in its hock-shaped bottle it is the perfect accompaniment to most of the dishes on the menu and can stand on its own feet if you fancy a drink after a swim. There is an extensive terrace with good views and a bar which is well-stocked and welcoming.

"Why do people come to São Brás ?, we asked the director. "Peace," replied Senhor Leite without hesitation. He is right. It is hard to imagine anything more restful and yet accessible than the Pousada at São Brás de Alportel. Incidentally, 'alportel' is Moorish for 'gateway'. If you pass through its entrance, you won't forget or regret it.

HOW TO FIND

Fairly easy. S. Brás is 30 kms north of Faro (on the Algarve coast). Take the main Lisbon road from S. Brás. After 2 kms there is a small road off to the right which goes to the pousada.

Tel: **(089) 842305/6**
Fax: **(089) 841726** Telex: **56945**

FACILITIES

RECREATION

GRADE

Top left: *Almond blossom heralds early Spring.* MK
Top right: *Algarve has some of Europe's finest golf courses.* MK
Bottom: *The pousada.* E

INFANTE • SAGRES

THE AREA

This is the most south-westerly point in Europe. Like many promotories in the south-west of other European countries it is shaven by the prevailing wind. It is bare, barren, blustery and bleak; yet it has a strange, severe and haunting beauty. In the calm, summer months the stillness and tranquility and the friendly, sparkling sea are a welcome interlude. In the winter the wind whistles across the empty plains and the sea snarls and thrashes the giant cliffs with an awe-inspiring ferocity. Spume is flung high into the cloudy sky and shipping keeps well off the point. The scene then is the antithesis of the holidaymaker's dream.

The attraction of Sagres is in its history. It was here that Prince Henry (*Infante* means king's son) founded his Navigation School at the beginning of the 15th century. His discoveries were to change the world. He was a son of King John I and born at Oporto. If you are British, you may be proud of the fact that his grandfather was John of Gaunt. Dom Henrique, Prince Henry the Navigator, the third of six sons, stands out as one of the most gifted, dedicated and intellectual men of all time. He was a genius.

From this very spot, as you sip your Sagres beer, remember he planned expeditions which prodded and probed their way down the west coast of Africa, then westwards into the unknown. Madeira was discovered in 1420 and Azores in 1431. Both are still Portuguese. They became staging posts, like the Canaries, on the way to America. Vasco da Gama rounded the Cape of Good Hope in 1498. He felt his way up the east coast of Africa before striking out again, once more into

the unknown, but this time to the east. He reached India and it is no coincidence that Bombay is so named. It is a corruption of the Portuguese bom baia (good bay). Goa, which has beaches to rival Portugal's, remained Portuguese for 14 years after India obtained independence from the British in 1947. Even Christopher Colombus had the good sense to marry a Portuguese and train at Sagres.

This part of Algarve is less populated and less popular than the resorts to the east. Burgau, Salema and the established Praia de Luz are fishing villages which have been corrupted by development but still retain some of their original charm. They all have good beaches.

Lagos (33 kms) is the nearest town and is a fairly easy 30 minutes by car along the RN 125 which is always being widened and improved. It is a port where many of the early caravels were built, and is very much a part of the history of the 'Discoveries'. Henry's statue stands in a square not far from the Praça da República where a well-preserved slave market (Mercado dos Escravos) is a timely reminder that not only gold, ivory and spices were brought back from newly-found lands across the seas.

Just round the corner from Henry's statue is the "golden" church of Santo António and a small museum full of fascinating archaeologically, historical and ethnic artifacts from the Algarve region.

Like many towns along the coastline of Algarve, tourism has done more for its prosperity than it has for its aesthetic appeal. Lagos has suffered less than many and the waterfront with a fort at the western end is attractive and full of atmosphere.

Top left: *Cataplana of pork and clams.* MK
Centre: *Algarve's south-west coast.* SR
Bottom right: *Europe's most south-westerly place of worship.* SR

There are plenty of restaurants and good shopping in an area largely restricted to pedestrians. A few pleasure yachts find their way into the harbour and the construction of a new marina will considerably enhance its popularity. As the sailors of today enter and leave with their charts, depth sounders, satellite navigators, radios and regular weather forecasts, let them offer thanks to Prince Henry who made it all happen.

INFANTE • SAGRES

THE POUSADA

This purpose-built pousada has a superb position on the cliff-top overlooking Sagres fort and, a little further up the coast, the Cape St. Vincent lighthouse. It was one of the early pousadas and since its erection in 1960 it has been considerably improved and upgraded. It now has a swimming pool and tennis court. There is a new bar, the theme of its decor being influenced by the maritime events which took place near here. Drake, Rodney, Nelson and Napier all fought major sea batles off Sagres.

The whole of the pousada is kept immaculately and the food, particularly the fish courses, are of a high standard. There is an à la carte in addition to the set menu. Often included are Pescada Grelhada com Molho de Manteiga (grilled buttered hake), Posta de Cherne (similar to halibut), Solha à Grenoblesa (plaice, though sometimes wrongly translated as sole), Linguado Grelhado com Molho de Manteiga (grilled buttered sole), and Espardarte no Forno (baked swordfish). They also do a good fish soup and their spinach and turnip soups are a little unusual. There is a mouth-watering sweet trolley with almond tart a great favourite.

The wine list is extensive with twenty-two reds (six in half bottles), twenty-two whites and six vinho verdes. French champagnes are on sale, but a very drinkable substitute at one-fifth of the price is Aliança Extra Bruto. There is a house wine from nearby Lagos and some from Lagoa further along the coast. Neither produce wines of the quality found in other parts of Portugal. Try the Bairradas or Dãos in either white or red. Sogrape and José Maria da Fonseca are very reliable producers, but there are many others.

There are some good naval prints scattered throughout the pousada and a portrait of Prince Henry looks down benignly from the wall of the reception-room. There are also a couple of good modern tapestries by Cãndido Costa Pinto.

The nearby fort and site of Henry's Navigation School with its huge compass rose are disappointing. They are badly maintained, with no information about the great deeds of the past. There used to be a small cinema showing the exploits of these great men, but it shut down four or five years ago. Unless you have visited the

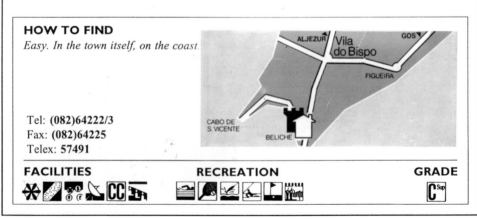

HOW TO FIND

Easy. In the town itself, on the coast.

Tel: **(082)64222/3**
Fax: **(082)64225**
Telex: **57491**

FACILITIES   **RECREATION**   **GRADE**

The Algarve's west coast. LP

Top left and above: *The view from the dining-room* E

Maritime Museum in Lisbon or have read up the subject you will leave Sagres very little the wiser. This is a great pity. Visitors come from all over the world to see the beginning of Portugal's greatness. Someone of the calibre of Prince Henry is badly needed to organise the place and present the full story of the 'Discoveries' to a public frustrated in its search for knowledge.

The beaches are sheltered if the wind is off the land, but otherwise they can be pretty draughty. There are good sands and several little beach restaurants serving fresh fish. 'O Telheiro' on Praia da Mareta is as good as any. The area is excellent for bird watching and fishing. There is a small harbour and a bay where dinghy sailing and wind-surfing are both popular. Whether you are studying birds nesting in the cliffs

or looking at the shipping rounding Cape St Vincent, a pair of binoculars is an advantage.

The lighthouse is one of the strongest in Europe with a beam of 32 sea miles. East are the pleasure beaches of Algarve stretching to Faro just over 100 kilometres away, and beyond. On a clear night you can pick out the lights of Lagos, Portimão and Carvoeiro. To the west lies the open sea. Travel due west and you hit the American coast not far south of New York, more than 6,500 kilometres away. We accept this as a fact. Ships and planes shrink the distance between Europe and the New World. As you gaze from your pousada balcony, what lies beyond the western horizon is known and accepted as commonplace. It was not always so.

QUINTA DA ORTIGA · SANTIAGO DO CACÉM

THE AREA & POUSADA
Only 5 kms from the town of Santiago do Cacém, the area is described in the chapter on the pousada São Tiago. Quinta da Ortiga was acquired from the executors of the late owner in 1991 and after modernisation was opened to provide additional accommodation for the small and heavily booked pousada in the town. Increasingly Quinta da Ortiga is preferred by visitors who find the peace of a rural setting more than compensation for the five kilometres from the centre. It is rather difficult to find. Take the Sines road from near the town pousada. 5 kms along this road turn right on to a minor road - there is a sign but it is largely obscured by another one - and go under a tunnel (i.e. under the main road you have left). At the 'T' junction turn left; the tree-lined drive to the quinta is 100 metres on your right.

The quinta stands in its own grounds of 4 hectares (10 acres) and is surrounded by farming land. Its twelve bedrooms are very much in demand particularly at weekends. There is a delightful pool area and terrace which is a redesigning and rebuilding of the pool belonging to the old quinta. In a short time the intimate dining-room has gained a reputation for good food and wines. Bacalhau com natas (salted codfish with cream) and Bacalhau Soufflé are two ways of serving this national dish. Enchidos Mistos (mixed sausages) is another very Portuguese dish which we have not seen in other pousadas. There is a very adequate wine list and the advice of the staff is worth taking.

In the grounds is a tiny chapel in which previous owners have worshipped. There is also a riding stable and plans for a tennis court may have fructified by the time you stay. On our last visit work had not been started.

For travellers who enjoy an isolated country house atmosphere with good amenities, you need look no further that Quinta da Ortiga.

Opposite: *The pousada.* E

HOW TO FIND
Tricky. Off the Santiago - Sines road. See text.

Tel: **(069) 22871**
Fax: **(069) 22073**

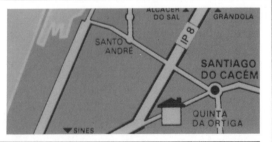

FACILITIES	RECREATION	GRADE
		B

STA. CRISTINA · CONDEIXA-A-NOVA

THE AREA

The improved IC2 and IP3 roads north of Coimbra (15 kms) and the IC3 south of Condeixa give easy access to this part of Portugal. Incidentally, IP is an abbreviation of *Itinerário Principal* and IC of *Itinerário Complementar,* the latter being usually an alternative route, in this case to the north / south A1 trunk road. The scenery may not have the grandeur of the Douro and Minho, but the countryside off the IC3 to Tomar is charming with a mix of vine, fruit, olive and colourful gardens or window boxes en route. Local crafts, which continue to flourish, include basket-making, weaving and hand-made tin cans of one sort or another, often for milk where plastic has not yet usurped the earlier craft. Bagpipes are still made in Coimbra, and old university town with a growing population, currently of about 70,000.

The guide books deal fairly fully with Coimbra but the university, founded in 1290 by King Dinis, must not be missed. The library is a baroque jewel dating from 1717 and the students are an interesting cross section of Portuguese youth. At one time undergraduates wore long black capes. Each rip in the cape represented a romantic conquest. Judging by the tattered state of these *capas* when I first saw them some thirty years ago, the scholastic calender must have been rather more erogenous than academic.

The Portuguese are justifiably proud of the river Mondego on which Coimbra stands. Unlike the other three great rivers, the Tagus, the Douro and the Minho, it owes none of its existence to Spain. It is Portuguese from beginning to end; from its source in the Serra da Estrela to the sea at Figueira da Foz. You may consider a river trip on the newly-built

'Basófias' which makes morning and evening excursions of about 1 hour 15 minutes. You can dine on board. The sound of music across the water recalls the fact that poets and writers have extolled the virtues of Coimbra and the Mondego. Coimbra *Fado* is reckoned to be the purest. A fado group made up of former graduates, often seen on television, are in a class of their own.

North of Coimbra is the Buçaco National Park and the top rate spa of Luso. Nearer to the pousada is the ancient settlement of Conimbriga (2 Kms) where, in the last years B.C., the Romans took possession of a former Iron Age settlement. It lay on the road from Lisbon to Braga via Tomar and a section of the highway is visible on the site. The mosaic floors which have been uncovered and restored since the excavations started in 1964 are exceptional. It is a National Monument and there is ample available literature in the adjoining museum. There is a restaurant and picnic area.

Opposite: *Conimbriga Roman ruins.* SR

STA.CRISTINA · CONDEIXA-A-NOVA

THE POUSADA

This 45-room pousada was opened at the end of 1993. It is of the standard of a five-star hotel with lifts, swimming pool and tennis courts. It occupies the site of the Palácio dos Almadas dating back to the 14th century. King Manuel I is reputed to have stayed here en route to Santiago de Compostela in 1514. It was redeveloped over the centuries and razed by the French in 1811. It was in a similar state of ruin when ENATUR took on the task of reconstructing the palace. Their architects are to be congratulated on the achievement. The buildings are still pristine and may lack the character and established shabby charm of the older Palácio Sotto Mayor opposite, but it is an extremely comfortable pousada in which an atmosphere of opulence has been created, in part by the inclusion of wall panels and other period features removed from distinguished buildings in Lisbon and elsewhere.

From the moment of your reception by Conceição or Maria João you will feel that your arrival matters. It takes time for a new pousada to become known and the occupancy rate, apart from weekends when business people from Coimbra and Viseu nearly fill the place, is little more than 20%. It is unrealistic to imagine that a chef can produce the entire à la carte menu at the drop of a hat when he knows that only a few tables in the dining room will be occupied. If you decide on something special, order in advance when having a pre-dinner drink. The cooking is good and the set menu changes daily. Included on the list are Arroz de Polvo (octopus rice), Tibornada de Bacalhau (codfish in a bread and oil stew - better than it sounds!), Cabrito Assado com Migas de Grelos (roasted kid with breadloaf), Ensopado de Enguias (eel stew) and, a great favourite of our's, Truta recheada com Presunto (grilled trout with bacon stuffing).

There is an increasing tendency to standardise the wine list throughout the chain but, in addition, each pousada has an individual selection of regional wines. We are now in the Bairrada wine district and it is difficult to go wrong. In our view Bairrada produces the best and the most reliable of Portuguese wines. The Vinho Pousadas de Portugal from the Mealhada Cooperative, in either white or red at 850 escudos, is a perfectly drinkable and very reasonably priced table wine. We recommend it. Two

---

HOW TO FIND

No problems. On the west side of the main road which runs parallel to the new IP 1 (A 1).

Tel: **(039) 941286**
Fax: **(039) 943097**

FACILITIES

RECREATION

GRADE

other Bairradas for your list are Frei João and Luís Pato.

There is a good rear terrace overlooking lawns and the swimming pool and several of the bedrooms have individual terraces. The layout makes this pousada very suitable for conferences or conventions and when it is better known the occupancy rate will improve materially. It is convenient for visiting the Conimbriga site and for Coimbra. It will prove to be an increasingly popular stopping place with a high standard of food and comfort.

Above: *The pousada. E*
Right: *Washing day. SR*

SÃO MIGUEL · SOUSEL

THE AREA

Being only 20 kms from the Pousada Rainha Santa Isabel at Estremoz, much that has been written in the chapter on that pousada applies equally to Sousel. It is a good centre for exploring Alentejo and in addition to the information given regarding the Estremoz and Évora pousadas, there are a number of other points of interest if you have the time.

Every effort should be made to visit nearby Avis because it was here that the House of Avis started. It ruled Portugal until 1580. The castle was built in the first part of the 13th century by a military order from Spain which subsequently was known as the Knights of Avis. João I was Grand Master of the Order before coming to the throne and marrying Philippa of Lancaster in 1385. Both castle and convent are sadly neglected by this hillside country town has an atmosphere in which it is not difficult to imagine past glories.

There are many feast days, particularly around the Easter period, which take place in the adjoining villages of Benavila, Cabeço de Vide, Fronteira and Santo Amaro. If you are interested, the local townhall can give you details. Perhaps the most unusual festival takes place adjoining the pousada. A minute and ancient bullring is the scene of festivities in honour of Nossa Senhora do Carmo da Serra. The *corridas* (bullfights) are staged on Easter Monday and it is the only time this isolated bullring is used. If bullfighting is not for you, there is quite a lot else going on and a pause in the little chapel next to the ring refreshes mind and body on a hot day. Cabeço de Vide is also a spa, although a poor relation of the larger Castelo de Vide further north. The railway station at Cabeço de Vide is a surprise. It is prolifically decorated with tiled panels *(azulejos)* telling the story of country life in these parts. It warrants a stop if you are travelling on EN 369.

The country surrounding the hill on which the pousada is built always seems greener than elsewhere in Alentejo due, of course, to the ample water from streams like the Vide, Sousel, Almadaye, Avis and Seda and to the man-made lake at Maranhão. Around Easter is a good time to see storks nesting in seemingly exposed and precarious places. There are plenty of egrets, magpies and jays about too.

Below: *Sunflower field.* SR

Opposite: *Fields of poppies and olives.* LP

SÃO MIGUEL · SOUSEL

THE POUSADA

The description "a rustic country house ideal for lovers of hunting..." given by ENATUR and travel agencies is misleading. It conjures up a picture of an old mature building - a shooting lodge for example. Nothing could be further from the truth. It is in fact a new building which was inaugurated by Portugal's Prime Minister Cavaco Silva in September 1992, although it was not until 1993 that the pousada was running smoothly and workmen were off the site. The swimming pool is still not completed. It is an interesting development by ENATUR and local businessmen who have combined to form ENASEL, which will promote country sports like shooting and fishing. In fact the pousada is well equipped to provide for these sports with kennels, cleaning rooms and gun and rod storage facilities.

You may be assured that if local dignitaries interested in hunting are involved, the food will be good. Certainly the Sunday buffet lunch is a banquet by any standards. The last time we were there the menu included 19 different dishes. The accent was naturally on local game and fish, and the duck and pheasant pate were first rate. Other dishes that remain in the memory are Feijoada de Lebre (hare), Bacalhau Espiritual (special dried codfish - much tastier than it sounds), Perdiz na Púcara (partridge) and Pèzinhos de coentrada (pork in a coriander sauce).

This modern building occupies a commanding position on a hilltop 3 kms from the country town of Sousel. There are 28 double bedrooms, four suites and a restaurant seating 200 people. The adjoining bullring and tiny chapel give an unique setting with impressive views over the surrounding Alentejo plains.

If you are keen on shooting or coarse fishing on the Maranhão dam you will find the management helpful in arranging this for you providing you can show evidence of your proficiency.

There are now so many pousadas in Alentejo that one is perhaps spoiled for choice. Sousel with its sporting facilities is a little different from the others.

Opposite: The pousada. E

HOW TO FIND

Care needed. Turn west in Sousel on the Cano - Casa Branca road. Almost immediately turn left. Aim for the summit of a prominent nearby hill (3 kms).

Tel: **(068) 551160**
Fax: **(068) 551155**

FACILITIES

RECREATION

GRADE

C Sup

MONSANTO

THE AREA

The countryside to the south and east is more fertile and attractive than to the north where it is strewn with boulders until the Serra da Malcata is reached. This vast area is now a National Park.

Monsanto is a corruption of Monte Santo (Holy hill). This commanding and rocky eminence has views across to Spain which is only 20 kms to the east. Away to the north-west the rising sun sparkles on the snow clad upper slopes of the Serra da Estrela as late as Easter.

Monsanto was given by King Afonso Henriques to The Knight Templar Gualdim de Pais in 1165. Originally a strategic castle against invaders, the subsequent centuries saw houses springing up around the military defences, some built into the rock face. Many of the cottages are hewn out of huge boulders with little pocket handkerchiefs as gardens where chickens and primulas compete for pride of place. It really is an enchanting spot. It is often described as the 'most typical village in Portugal', but nothing could be further from the truth. It is unique.

With its fame, crowds are attracted. The height of the holiday season, when parking becomes a problem, is not the best time to enjoy the tiny alleys and minute squares. Spring or autumn, or even a good spell in the winter, is the ideal time to appreciate both the village and the outlook. The local authority, ever mindful of the comfort of its visitors, has erected a public lavatory which must have the best views of any public lavatory in the world.

MONSANTO

Any number of the surrounding villages have good examples of 17th and 18th century Beira houses with steps leading up to the first floor verandah and entrance porch, often decorated with a nobleman's coat of arms. Village pillories, now more often in granite than marble, can be seen at Penha Garcia and Idanha-a-Velha. Idanha-a-Velha should be included in your itinerary. Like Monsanto, it is a picture postcard village with great scope for the photographer. It was occupied by the Romans. Excavations, funded by the Gulbenkian Institute, have taken place in, under and around the abandoned church, the nave of which is now an interesting museum of artefacts uncovered during archeological digs. What a benefactor Gulbenkian has proved to be to Portugal.

For visitors who like larger towns, Castelo Branco (45 kms) is preferable to Fundão. The centre is well laid out with shady gardens and cafés. The museum is housed in the old bishop's palace with a typical 'Beira' entrance. Not only is the building worth seeing in its own right, but the surrounding formal gardens make a perfect setting. On the first floor is the embroidery school - Escola de Bordados Regionais do Museu de Francisco Tavares Proença.

THE POUSADA

This small pousada (10 rooms) was opened at the end of 1993. It honoured a promise. In 1938, during the Salazar regime, Monsanto was presented with a golden cockerel. It acknowledged the dictator's passion for what he considered to be the loveliest village in Portugal. "In making this award to the village of Monsanto I wish you to ensure a pousada is built to encourage visitors." Almost sixty years later, under a democratic government, the wish became a reality. A replica of the golden cockerel surmounts the clock tower. Of the ten rooms, two face the surrounding countryside and the others overlook the village. Room 103 with a small terrace is the best. There is a lift and an intimate dining-room. The menu is changed daily and the food is of a good standard. Our party had Arroz de Pato (duck rice) and Cabrito assado com Migas e molho picante (roast kid with a spicy sauce). This was preceeded by an excellent cream of vegetable soup and followed by a selection of local cheeses, a sweet trolley and coffee. All agreed it was outstanding value. Isabel waited at table and we took her recommendation on wines - a red from Fundão, Praça Velha. In Isabel this isolated pousada has an

employee who makes the waiters at some of the Chateau category pousadas look pedestrian. Cora da Beira and Conde Julião are other local wines.

The wall coverings are worthy of mention. the largest is from Castelo Branco and is in delicately worked silk. These panels are not cheap. This particular one would be worth about 1,500,000 escudos. Demand outstrips supply and over the years Castelo Branco embroidery and Arraiolos carpets have proved sound and pleasurable investments.

The director is a professional with considerable experience in other pousadas. He is a great believer that when a customer ceases to be called by his name and becomes merely a room number the whole spirit of the pousada has been lost. In the lowest category of the pousada range, this pousada offers very good value with a welcoming and friendly atmosphere.

Pages 158 - 63: *Views of Monsanto.* SR/E

HOW TO FIND
Easy. In the centre of this mountain village. Watch out for hairpin bends. Limited car-parking.

Tel: **(077) 32425/6**
Fax: **(077) 32432**

FACILITIES	RECREATION	GRADE
		B

CASTELO DE ALVITO

THE AREA

Alvito is in the heartland of Alentejo where summer temperatures are merciless. Air conditioning in car and home, if not essential, is highly desirable. The best time to explore the infectious charm of Alentejo is in the spring or autumn, and even a dry spell in the winter has much to commend it. Sadly, it is not possible to select a dry week or fortnight a couple of months in advance when planning a holiday.

Alvito is 241 metres above sea level, although the commanding views across the plains to Beja give the impression that it is much higher. It is close to the river Odivelas and 15 kms from the *barragem* (dam) of the same name. Although in high summer it is easy to get the impression that the area is dry and arid, there is ample water and this was one of the reasons the Romans encamped in these parts. Nowhere is this better illustrated than at Quinta de Água de Peixes (6 kms). It is signposted from the central square near the castle and a visit is recommended. Here is water in abundance which has been pouring into fountains and ornamental ponds for centuries. It comes from a prolific underground source. The property is privately owned and is not open to the public unless you are lucky enough to persuade the caretaker to give you access. We had no difficulty in looking around the gardens and enjoying the shade of the trees overhanging the ornamental waters that run the full length of the rear façade. This 15th century manor house is an oasis in the plains of Alentejo and it is to be hoped sufficient funds will be available to maintain the structure which is already showing signs of deterioration. It is owned by the Cambodolista family who

Opposite: *White stork & brood.* LP
Left and below bottom: *Quinta de Água de Peixes.* LP/SR
Page 166: *S. Cucufate ruins.* LP
Pages 167/9: *The pousada.* LP/E

CASTELO DE ALVITO

inherited the manor. Some guide books give the owners as the banking family Espírito Santo, but this is incorrect. The architecture is an interesting mix of Moorish, as seen in the window arches, Manuelino and Gothic.

Drive your car in any direction, take the minor roads, and you will discover a way of life which has moved into the 20th century with reluctance. Local crafts include good leather work and in nearby Cuba we found a beautifully made montage of every conceivable farm instrument cleverly executed to scale with the Portuguese name of each piece below. You can see them in Senhor António Paquete's Café Central in Rua Serpa Pinto.

Take the opportunity of visiting the Roman ruins at Vila de Frades. Leave Alvito on the Vidigueira (EN 258) road and a little before Vila de Frades there is a sign on the left-hand side of the road indicating the site.

This Roman manor house which subsequently became the monastery of S. Cucufate was neglected until French and Portuguese archaeologists recently excavated the site. The place had been ransacked and even dynamited in order to obtain brickwork for use on other buildings. It is now a national monument and the uncovering of religious wall paintings is a work of art in itself. *Tesouros Artísticos de Portugal* stated that King Afonso III gave the ancient monastery to the Canons of the Order of S. Vicente de Fora in Lisbon and that subsequently it passed to Vasco da Gama in 1519. As Vasco da Gama died in Índia in 1524, he could not have had much benefit from his ownership.

In considering places of interest we suggest you refer to the other pousadas situated in Alentejo. None of them is an impossible distance by car.

CASTELO DE ALVITO

THE POUSADA
The castle of Alvito was opened as a pousada at the end of 1993. As you enjoy a drink in the courtyard, it is interesting to reflect on its history. In 1482 King Afonso V gave permission for the 1st Baron and Lord of Alvito to build a castle here. Before he was created Baron, Senhor João da Silveira had held many government posts, including Secretary of State and Inspector of the Treasury. It was unique for a private individual to own a castle at that time; they were all in royal ownership. Through the centuries many kings and queens of Portugal have stayed here and it was a place of importance and prestige. However, by the end of the 19th century the castle was abandoned and became the home of gypsy squatters. The House of Bragança Foundation rescued the castle from further neglect and it is the Foundation who have granted a lease for an initial period of 25 years for the conversion of the pousada we know today. The architect has done a good job combining all the modern accoutrements without detracting from the ambience of the past.

There are 20 bedrooms, a lift, good reception rooms and a dining room seating 100.

Outside there are gardens with a swimming pool and a little amphitheatre. As with all new ventures there are teething troubles. Staff in these remote areas need training and are not easy to find. The director, Senhor Domingos Lameira, who was born in Elvas and knows Alentejo well, has been quick to spot the weaknesses. Standards on our last visit were much improved.

This is a wine area and the wines from Vidigueira, Redonda and Reguengos are all excellent. The Pousada Red and White are good choices and unless you have any particular preference you will not regret a bottle. It is in fact another Alentejo wine, specially bottled for the Pousada at Borba.

The food although somewhat limited in choice is well prepared. Vitela Estufada (veal stew), Carne de Porco com coentros (pork with coriander) and Borrego Assado (roast lamb) are reliable choices. For fish lovers, Peixe Assado (oven-roasted fish) and Caldeirada de Bacalhau com Ervas Aromáticas (codfish stew flavoured with herbs from the garden) are recommended. Before leaving Alentejo, experiment with the local soup, Açorda à Alentejana. It is a garlic flavoured clear soup with bread and a poached egg.

HOW TO FIND
Easy. In the centre of this small country town.

Tel: (084) 48383
Fax: (084) 48383

FACILITIES

RECREATION

GRADE

CH

UPDATE

TEMPORARY CLOSURES IN 1994 AND 1995

ENATUR has embarked upon a major programme to expand, modernise and refurbish many of the pousadas. This means that in the second half of 1994 and in 1995 works will be in progress at some pousadas which remain open, while others will be temporarily closed. The ones most likely to be closed for periods of several months are Santa Clara, Vale do Gaio, São Bartolomeu, Barão Forrester, São Bras and São Tiago.

It is important when making a booking for any of the pousadas to check the current position regarding works. This can be done by:

Telephone - (01) 8481221, 8489078 or 8484602

Fax - (01) 805846 or 8484349

Telex - 63475 ENATUR P

Mail - ENATUR, Av. Santa Joana a Princessa 10A, 1700 Lisboa.

MORE POUSADAS TO OPEN BY END OF 1994

At the time of writing, three pousadas are in the course of construction. They are due to open by the end of 1994, but you are urged to check the latest situation with the Central Reservation Office in Lisbon (fax and phone as above).

At this stage we can only comment on the buildings, their location and our suggestions on things worth seeing in the area. We look forward to sampling the cuisine and comfort of each one in due course so that the next edition will have more detailed comments.

At the moment, they are unborn babies yet to see the light of day and to be christened. Some may criticise the pousadas for one reason or another, but all must agree that Portugal has some very fine architects and those commissioned for the conversion and building of the pousada chain are among the best. All three of these new pousadas will be in the top (Chateau) category. Two of them, Beja and Crato, are in the Alentejo.

Queluz is 13 kms NW from the centre of Lisbon. With the opening of Beja and Crato, Alentejo will provide the traveller with a choice of eleven pousadas. It will open up this largest but little explored province where hitherto hotel accommodation has been sparse.

Beja's Convento de S.Francisco will welcome restoration. It has had a checkered career since its foundation in the 13th century, ending up after 1834 as barracks. Hopefully the kitchens will better the army rations served here in the past! Sister Mariana of the other convent in Beja - Convento de Conceição had an even more checkered career. She had a long running *affaire* with the Marquis de Saint-Léger whilst he was serving as a French colonel in the war against Spain in 1661-1668.

Beja, an old Roman town, is today the centre of Alentejo's agriculture. The approach across the plains is to experience the vastness of Alentejo. In the stillness of a summer's day, interrupted momentarily by a low-flying fighter jet from the local airforce base as it streaks across the blue sky, is to feel the atmosphere of this lonely, sparsely populated province. The rather clumsy tower of the castle looms out of the haze. In the heat of a Portuguese summer the highest temperatures in the country are recorded here. Not far from the Convento de S.Francisco is the Tourist Office with pamphlets on local events.

The pousada will have 37 rooms, a restaurant seating 150 and rooms suitable for conferences. In addition to the drawing-room, terrace and bar, there will be a tennis court and chapel. Perhaps of even greater benefit to visitors, especially in the hot months, will be the swimming pool. It will be interesting to see the décor and soft furnishings of the interior and whether they can rival the standards already set in the established Chateau pousadas of Évora and Estremoz.

Mosteiro de Flor da Rosa, Crato is situated about 20 kms to the west of Portalegre, a charming and spacious town. This is an area of intense historical interest. Flor da Rosa, a fortified monastery lying a couple of kilometres to the north of Crato, dates from 1358 when it was founded by Brother Álvaro Pereira. He is best remembered as the father of Condestável Nuno Álvares Pereira who, with a substantially inferior force, gave the Spaniards such a bloody nose at the Battle of Aljubarrota (see Batalha pousada). By far the most intriguing character in these parts was the last Bishop of Crato. There is no reference to him in most guide books and Fodor's tells us he was the illegitimate son of King Pedro. As there was no king of this name on the throne for the previous two hundred years this is obviously nonsense. António, Prior of Crato,

became King of Portugal for a day in 1580. João III's successors were unable to sustain the direct line to the throne. Sebastião, his son, spent most of this time, money and army fighting an abortive war in Africa where he was killed. His uncle Henrique, the Cardinal-King, took over but died childless. It seemed inevitable that the throne would pass to Spain. António, however, claimed he was the illegitimate son of João III's brother Prince Luís and his mistress Violante Gomes. He had himself proclaimed king but his success was short-lived. He had one further attempt nine years later with British support but was equally unsuccessful. Portugal remained under Spanish rule for 60 years until the powerful House of Bragança established independence.

Archeologists have done a lot of work in and around the monastery and it is hoped to establish a small museum to exhibit their finds. The pousada will have 24 bedrooms of which seven will be in the original structure. The dining-room on the first floor will command good views across the countryside and a swimming pool will welcome visitors after wearying journeys across these historical plains. Architect Carrilho da Graça has immense opportunities to bring into the 20th century this ancient monument. We are looking forward to spending a night or two there.

Palácio de Queluz is the nearest pousada to the centre of Lisbon (13 kms). It is arguable whether a hotel in the town's centre is the place to stay to explore the capital. If you find the bustle and traffic roar of a metropolis to your liking then there are any number of good hotels available. If, on the other hand, you enjoy exploring the sights and sounds of Lisbon but prefer to escape to a quieter atmosphere at the end of what can be a tiring day, then Queluz is for you. In making your decision bear in mind that the communications from Queluz to the centre are excellent. There is a good motorway road and plenty of taxis which are still cheaper than in other capital cities of Europe. There are also train and bus connections, details of which you may get from Reception. Unfortunately, 'bag-snatching' is becoming all too common on public transport. Be warned. Staying at Queluz makes a visit to the other palaces of Sintra and Ajuda very easy and they are not to be missed. Both Queluz and Ajuda are used for the reception of foreign dignitaries but, like Sintra, are open to the public. They also house some exceptional exhibitions from time to time.

The palace was built in the second half of the 18th century by King Pedro III (then a prince) who married his niece (Queen Maria I). She was a devout catholic who sadly developed religious mania and died here. The pousada is being constructed in the part of the palace known as the Torre do Relógio. The architects, Fernando Mendes and Carlos Ramos, have accepted a real challenge. Their work will stand alongside the brilliance of Mateus Vicente de Oliveira and the Frenchman Jean Baptiste Robillon, who were the original creators of both the palace and gardens, and the architects who were responsible for the sympathetic restoration after a fire in 1934 had badly damaged the original.

There will be 27 bedrooms, a drawing-room, breakfast-room and a small theatre. The restaurant to the pousada will be the already long-established Cozinha Velha located in the Palace of Queluz.

There is nothing heavy or overpowering about Queluz. It is not a Vila Viçosa or a Mafra. It has a French lightness and frivolity sobered by its formal gardens. The British Royal family, including the Queen and Prince Phillip, have been guests here.

GETTING UNDERWAY

Having decided on Portugal, one of the first things to think about is how to get there: by air, by land or by land and sea? Many airlines fly either scheduled or charter services to the country's three mainland airports: Lisbon, Oporto and Faro. Within Portugal, travel by car is by far the best way of seeing the country. Travel agents can couple flight reservations with arrangements for a hire car to be available at the airport upon your arrival. Remember to take your driving licence; either national or international will do.

If you intend using a private vehicle, make sure the registration and insurance documents are in order. Take along a letter of authorisation from the owner, preferably translated into Portuguese, if the vehicle is not registered in your name. The drive from all mainland European countries is via Spain. It is straightforward. Travel by car from the United Kingdom involves a sea passage, of course. Your options: the most convenient English channel crossing, or the longer Brittany Ferries route from Plymouth to Santander on Spain's north coast. Tickets for the latter are obviously more expensive, but then you cut down on petrol, accommodation en route and driving time on the Continent. Information on all aspects of car travel and frontier crossings can be obtained from motoring organisations in your own country, or by writing to the Automóvel Club de Portugal, Rua Rosa Araujo 24, Lisbon.

Next to be decided is when to travel. When temperatures are quoted they are often *average* temperatures, therefore there are some substantially hotter days in the summer and some substantially colder and wetter days in the winter. Unless you have an air-conditioned car, our advice would be to keep away from the southern half of the country in the last week of July, August and the first week of September. The weather apart, the majority of Portuguese seem to favour August as the holiday month. Statistically it is a fact that the standard of driving is lower in Portugal than elsewhere in Europe. This is another reason for avoiding the busy hot months. The north of Portugal is cooler than the south as you will see by looking at the temperatures for Oporto. Freezing conditions may be met in the Serra da Estrela and the highlands of Trás-os-Montes during the winter months. The wettest months are November and December. During the other winter months there is often rain interspersed with sun and blue skies. The climate sometimes changes very quickly and a ghastly damp, dull day in winter can be followed by spring-like weather.

The table giving distances and driving times between pousadas is based on an average of 60 kms per hour on normal roads and 40 kms on mountainous roads. Studying this table should persuade you that unless your stay is for more than a month it is not possible to see all of Portugal. It is not a very big country, but if some of the places mentioned in each chapter are to be explored without a mad rush, the country divides itself into two halves. Roughly, the dividing line connects the pousadas of Batalha, Castelo de Bode (Tomar) and Marvão. North of this line there are 17 pousadas and south of it there are 16. In the southern half, of course, is Lisbon which is one of the loveliest capitals in Europe. It would be a great pity to miss it when doing the southern tour. Sadly, as yet there is no pousada in the capital, but there is a good selection of hotels.

NORTHERN TOUR

On a fly/drive visit, Oporto is a good starting point. If you are driving your own car, there are many frontier points of entry, either across the river Minho in the extreme north or on the eastern boundary with Spain, including the major one at Vilar Formoso. The merits of Almeida às a place to unwind is mentioned under the chapter on Senhora das Neves. This could be followed by some mountain scenery at Manteigas, then Oliveira do Hospital and on to Serem and Aveiro. Head up north to the border town of Valença or Vila Nova de Cerveira; south to the mountain retreat of Caniçada, south again to Guimarães (two pousadas to choose from); across country to Alijó to learn all about port wine, before making for the outpost of Miranda do Douro. This invloves a minimum of 10 pousadas. Two nights in each, or certainly in some of them, and perhaps one in Oporto (where the stock exchange must not be missed) and all too quickly a three-week holiday has disappeared. This is why it is best to have two bites at the cherry by coming back next year and taking a more southerly route.

SOUTHERN TOUR

A fly/drive tour would start either at Lisbon or Faro. Arriving by road, there are several frontier crossings along Portugal's eastern border, the main three being on the road to Elvas from Badajoz, the road to Serpa from Aracena, and - the most southerly - either by ferry or the new bridge at Vila Real de Santo António.

The point of arrival will decide the sequence of visits. Clockwise from Faro we suggest São Brás de Alportel as a good stop to 'get the feel of things' and relax before moving on to Sagres. Travel north to Santiago de Cacém and north again to either Setúbal or Palmela. Take the motorway over the Tagus Bridge to Lisbon, which warrants two nights. Drive across country to the three 'E's - Évora, Estremoz and Elvas though miss the last one unless you are arriving or leaving by this frontier crossing. Head south now through the heart of Alentejo to Serpa and then south again to Faro with perhaps a night en route at Sao Brás.

CENTRAL TOUR

It will be noted that the central dividing line of pousadas has not been included in either of the above itineraries. Once again it is a question of time. Time permitting, they can be incorporated in either one or other of the tours suggested above. In point of fact they make a very natural visit on their own. This is because a central tour should include Lisbon, Alcobaça, Batalha and Tomar all of them absolute MUSTS but nevertheless time consuming if they are to be appreciated to the full. A suggestion for the fly/driver starting from Lisbon would be two nights in the capital; then, Obidos (just south of Caldas da Rainha on the map); north-east to Batalha, stopping on the way to look at Alcobaça; east after Batalha to Tomar (Castelo-de Bode) passing Fatima en route; and east again to Marvão, checking first to see that the redevelopment has been completed. If not, there are hotels in the spa town of Castelo de Vide which is interesting and a convenient spot to turn south for the two lovely Alentejo pousadas at Estremoz and Évora. Thence, sadly, back to Lisbon and the plane home.

Portuguese and foreign residents in Portugal have the opportunity to enjoy the countryside as and when the opportunity and the desire strikes. A weekend's skiing is not an impossibility when conditions are right. For those lucky enough to live permanently in Portugal, this book will hopefully encourage visits to less familiar parts of the country.

NEW TOUR

The increasing number of new pousadas opened in 1993 and 1994 and planned for 1995 gives the traveller a wide choice. It has become increasingly difficult, if not impossible, to see all of the pousadas in a limited holiday period. By coincidence the new ones provide an interesting tour on their own.

Part of Queluz Palace should be open as a pousada and this makes an ideal starting point for Lisbon arrivals. Queluz is on the north-west fringe of Lisbon, 13 kms from the centre, and there is a good, fast road and ample taxis. It is a restful base from which to explore Lisbon and Sintra. The minimum stay is two nights.

After a massive cultural intake, a night or two in the country at Sousel, Alvito or Beja will recharge intellectual batteries before striking up north to the mountain village of Monsanto and, via Guarda and the IP5, IP3 and IC3, to the very comfortable Santa Cristina at Condeixa. The Roman ruins at Conimbriga can be seen on your return to Lisbon, which is better made on the IC3 than the motorway. It enables you to stop in Alpiarça to see Casa dos Patudos, the home of the wealthy José Relvas, now open as a museum.

Average monthly temperatures *(centigrade)*

maximum 11
minimum 6

	Centigrade	0		10		20		30
	Fahrenheit	32		50		68		86

	Jan	Feb	Mar	Apr	May	Jun	Jul	Aug	Sep	Oct	Nov	Dec
Oporto (max)	15	13	16	16	20	23	25	25	22	22	17	14
(min)	4	6	7	8	10	13	14	14	13	13	10	6
Lisbon (max)	15	15	16	18	22	25	28	28	25	24	19	15
(min)	7	9	9	10	13	15	18	17	16	16	12	9
Alentejo (max)	14	13	15	17	22	28	23	29	25	25	16	12
(min)	5	7	7	9	11	14	16	16	15	15	10	6
Faro (max)	16	16	17	19	23	25	28	28	26	24	19	17
(min)	6	9	9	11	13	16	18	18	16	15	12	8

Distances and driving times between the pousadas.

96 | *Distance in Kilometres*

1.40 | *Driving time in hours and/or minutes*

To calculate the driving time, an average speed of 40km/h on mountain roads and 60km/h on other roads has been considered.

BARÃO DE FORREST

STA. MARIN▮

SRA. DAS NEV▮

MESTRE AF. DOMINGUE▮

S. MIGUEL [2 | 3 …]

STA. CRISTINA [250 / 3.20] [1 …]

H. STA. LUZIA [230 / 3.00] [480 / 5.30] [5 …]

ORTIGA [560 / 6.30] [400 / 4.50] [170 / 2.50] [3 …]

CASTELO DO ALVITO [98 / 1.50] [471 / 6.40] [282 / 3.20] [82 / 1.30] [3 …]

S. FRANCISCO [32 / 0.40] [76 / 1.20] [504 / 6.10] [321 / 3.20] [121 / 1.30] [3 …]

MONSANTO [304 / 4.00] [246 / 3.20] [346 / 4.30] [456 / 5.30] [175 / 2.10] [177 / 2.15] [3 …]

FARO [462 / 5.00] [175 / 2.50] [196 / 2.30] [230 / 3.00] [650 / 7.00] [550 / 6.10] [310 / 4.10] […]

COIMBRA [454 / 6.00] [489 / 3.00] [333 / 4.15] [362 / 4.20] [415 / 4.50] [193 / 2.50] [15 / 0.20] [265 / 3.40] [1 …]

PORTO [117 / 1.40] [571 / 7.00] [303 / 4.00] [432 / 5.10] [462 / 6.00] [440 / 1.30] [71 / 2.10] [130 / 5.00] [387 / …] […]

LISBOA [313 / 3.50] [196 / 2.50] [300 / 3.40] [311 / 4.10] [186 / 3.00] [162 / 2.40] [150 / 2.40] [385 / 4.50] [183 / 2.50] [199 / …]

S. TEOTÓNIO																												
S. BENTO																												96 1.40
N. SRA. OLIVEIRA																											89 2.10	114 2.15
S. GONÇALO																										60 1.00	154 2.30	148 2.30
S. BARTOLOMEU																									142 1.50	220 3.00	230 5.00	326 5.30
STA. CATARINA																								83 1.00	184 2.30	289 3.50	309 5.00	405 5.30
RIA																							404 4.10	321 3.30	123 2.10	90 1.45	226 3.30	193 2.15
STO. ANTÓNIO																						51 0.45	285 3.00	299 3.20	137 2.15	88 1.40	177 2.40	182 2.45
S. JERÓNIMO																					56 0.50	108 1.30	251 2.50	285 3.00	156 2.00	136 2.00	225 3.20	213 3.00
STA. BÁRBARA																				74 1.10	92 1.20	155 2.00	230 2.50	220 2.30	175 2.30	156 2.20	245 3.50	272 3.45
S. LOURENÇO																			45 1.00	74 1.10	130 1.30	198 2.30	234 3.00	230 2.50	200 2.40	210 2.50	299 4.00	319 4.00
S. PEDRO																		197 2.30	150 2.10	153 2.30	148 2.00	194 2.15	340 4.00	360 4.00	216 2.50	197 2.50	286 4.00	306 3.40
CASTELO																	100 1.20	229 2.40	182 2.30	205 2.00	205 2.00	251 2.30	350 4.40	390 4.10	248 3.00	206 2.50	295 4.30	351 4.00
STA. MARIA																194 2.50	108 1.50	201 2.30	214 2.50	202 2.30	252 2.30	298 3.00	347 4.10	397 4.30	332 4.10	307 4.00	396 5.30	416 4.35
STA. LUZIA															75 1.20	245 3.20	152 2.10	255 3.00	277 3.00	252 2.30	302 3.00	348 3.40	427 5.00	477 5.00	387 4.40	363 4.50	452 5.15	472 5.15
RAINHA STA. ISABEL														54 0.50	77 1.20	191 2.50	161 2.20	260 3.00	278 3.00	253 2.40	303 3.00	349 3.40	457 5.00	446 5.00	436 5.00	376 5.00	465 5.00	495 5.00
LÓIOS													44 0.50	98 1.20	121 1.50	178 2.30	149 2.20	320 3.20	322 3.20	210 2.30	266 3.00	312 3.15	505 5.10	485 5.00	308 5.00	368 5.00	457 5.00	477 5.00
PALMELA												108 1.30	140 2.10	192 2.40	217 3.00	141 2.15	141 2.40	327 3.50	311 3.40	301 3.20	341 3.30	387 3.40	502 5.00	472 5.00	330 4.50	360 5.00	449 5.00	469 5.00
S. FILIPE											8 0.15	101 1.30	133 2.00	187 2.40	210 2.50	148 2.20	149 2.40	334 3.50	304 3.40	290 3.20	334 3.30	380 3.40	510 5.00	487 5.10	345 5.00	340 5.00	429 5.00	449 5.00
VALE DO GAIO										70 1.20	78 1.20	52 1.00	97 1.30	152 2.30	175 2.40	180 3.00	173 2.30	355 4.10	311 3.40	325 3.40	371 3.50	417 3.50	560 6.00	542 6.00	400 5.40	374 5.20	463 5.20	483 5.20
S. TIAGO									55 1.00	92 1.40	100 1.40	94 1.30	139 2.10	199 3.00	217 3.00	198 3.30	206 2.50	399 4.40	334 3.50	350 3.50	398 4.00	444 4.10	580 6.15	570 6.15	428 6.00	405 6.00	494 6.15	514 6.15
S. GENS								106 1.30	92 1.30	164 2.10	172 2.10	152 2.30	193 2.40	202 3.00	225 3.20	265 3.40	255 3.10	477 5.00	426 4.30	413 4.20	463 4.30	509 4.40	595 6.30	589 6.30	489 6.30	479 6.30	568 6.50	588 7.00
STA. CLARA							137 1.40	90 1.20	141 1.50	169 2.10	177 2.20	153 2.40	234 3.20	284 3.40	307 3.50	276 3.40	273 3.40	465 5.00	416 4.40	420 4.20	471 4.30	517 4.50	655 7.30	646 7.20	498 6.40	477 6.30	566 6.50	586 7.00
S. BRÁS						97 1.40	161 2.00	200 2.50	161 2.20	250 3.40	258 3.40	217 3.30	265 3.50	315 4.30	311 4.00	346 4.20	424 5.10	530 5.20	497 5.10	509 4.50	555 5.00	601 5.20	735 7.50	735 7.50	587 7.40	573 7.40	662 8.10	682 8.20
INFANTE					116 1.40	112 2.10	208 2.30	140 2.10	202 3.00	244 3.40	252 3.40	267 3.50	307 4.30	354 4.50	377 4.10	340 4.20	358 4.50	540 5.20	500 5.00	500 4.50	545 5.00	591 5.20	715 7.30	715 7.30	567 8.15	610 8.30	699 8.40	719 8.50
D. DINIS				703 8.50	663 6.50	601 6.30	597 6.40	527 6.10	507 6.00	477 5.50	469 5.40	532 5.40	507 5.40	514 5.40	443 5.00	374 4.40	349 4.20	303 3.00	278 3.00	256 2.40	200 2.30	184 1.40	370 5.00	330 5.00	169 2.00	108 1.50	100 1.50	16 0.25
			214 3.50	667 7.40	688 7.00	626 6.30	652 6.50	552 6.30	532 6.20	502 6.10	494 6.00	498 5.50	473 5.30	466 5.20	395 5.00	343 4.30	297 3.40	197 2.40	175 2.40	158 2.10	219 2.20	209 2.10	170 1.40	140 1.40	46 0.50	85 1.15	209 3.15	229 3.30
		88 1.30	111 2.00	613 7.40	678 7.40	479 6.20	481 6.00	396 5.40	376 5.30	372 5.20	364 5.10	372 4.30	379 4.30	366 4.30	310 3.40	210 3.00	201 3.10	220 3.00	224 3.00	150 2.00	111 1.40	101 1.30	250 3.00	220 3.00	59 1.00	4 0.10	100 2.30	116 2.30
	244 3.40	137 3.00	352 4.30	617 7.50	638 7.00	576 6.30	450 5.50	502 6.10	482 6.00	440 5.40	432 5.30	340 4.00	297 3.40	288 3.30	219 3.00	355 4.20	265 2.40	100 1.19	111 1.30	109 1.40	164 2.00	210 2.10	142 2.20	189 2.40	185 2.40	225 2.50	319 4.00	339 4.00
	189 2.40	282 4.20	435 5.00	335 3.50	356 3.50	294 3.30	281 3.30	220 3.00	199 2.50	169 2.30	161 2.20	228 3.10	208 3.10	225 3.20	171 2.50	50 0.50	67 1.10	153 2.00	132 1.50	154 1.50	155 1.50	201 2.15	405 4.00	375 4.00	233 3.00	187 2.40	290 3.30	301 3.40
	395 4.50	480 5.50	520 6.00	330 4.50	280 4.10	250 3.40	215 3.00	155 2.30	110 1.50	130 2.20	160 2.30	60 1.10	16 0.20	70 1.20	95 1.40	200 3.00	160 2.20	270 3.00	270 3.00	250 2.40	300 3.20	340 3.50	460 5.00	440 5.00	430 5.00	370 5.00	460 5.00	490 5.00
	190 2.40	210 2.40	290 3.10	458 5.50	520 6.00	380 4.50	370 4.30	350 4.30	270 3.30	250 3.10	250 3.10	250 3.10	260 3.20	250 3.10	200 2.50	150 2.00	100 1.40	100 1.40	100 1.40	70 1.10	70 1.10	100 1.30	290 3.50	280 3.50	130 1.50	120 2.00	210 3.20	250 3.00
	80 1.20	180 2.50	40 0.50	670 8.30	620 6.50	580 6.40	560 6.40	490 6.50	470 6.40	439 6.40	432 6.40	447 6.00	410 6.00	500 6.20	440 5.20	360 4.50	320 4.00	290 3.30	260 3.20	240 3.20	180 2.50	170 1.40	350 4.50	300 4.40	169 2.30	90 1.40	100 1.50	60 100
	410 5.50	560 6.50	540 650	140 2.10	200 3.00	100 1.40	120 1.40	9 0.15	60 1.00	100 1.40	104 1.40	100 1.40	145 2.10	210 3.00	220 3.10	230 3.40	215 3.00	410 5.00	340 4.00	360 4.10	405 4.50	450 5.10	600 6.50	580 6.30	435 6.20	510 6.10	560 7.00	590 7.00
	404 5.00	530 6.30	564 6.50	232 3.15	214 3.10	149 2.10	70 1.10	91 1.40	26 0.30	110 1.50	118 2.00	36 0.40	94 1.10	148 1.50	170 2.30	227 3.40	198 2.50	370 4.40	372 4.40	260 3.20	316 4.30	362 3.40	555 6.20	535 6.10	358 3.40	418 5.00	507 6.00	527 6.10
	489 5.20	509 6.20	540 6.50	290 4.10	150 1.30	130 1.20	28 0.30	75 1.10	92 1.40	140 2.10	148 2.20	78 1.20	122 1.10	176 2.40	193 3.00	280 4.30	245 4.10	300 3.00	304 3.00	440 5.00	361 3.40	371 3.50	544 6.20	545 6.20	540 6.20	489 5.50	529 6.10	556 6.30
	306 4.10	243 3.30	388 4.40	570 6.00	414 5.00	432 5.10	333 4.00	336 4.00	274 3.40	333 4.00	343 4.20	239 3.10	193 2.50	240 3.40	125 2.00	288 3.40	194 2.50	100 1.40	102 1.40	124 2.00	164 2.30	219 2.50	290 3.40	296 3.40	280 3.30	302 3.40	344 4.10	402 4.50
	690 7.50	710 7.50	690 7.20	116 1.40	20 0.15	117 1.50	180 2.10	220 3.00	170 2.20	270 3.50	278 3.50	237 3.30	285 3.50	335 4.40	331 4.30	366 4.30	444 5.10	550 5.30	510 5.40	520 5.00	570 5.30	620 5.40	750 8.10	750 8.10	600 8.00	590 8.00	680 8.30	700 8.40
	475 2.20	200 2.30	275 3.10	470 5.50	440 5.10	390 4.50	385 4.40	360 4.30	185 3.40	246 3.20	240 3.50	254 3.40	275 3.40	270 3.20	200 2.50	150 2.00	115 1.40	115 1.40	115 1.40	85 1.20	85 1.20	62 1.00	300 3.50	312 4.00	145 2.00	105 1.50	200 3.20	246 3.50
	52 1.00	159 2.00	108 1.20	577 6.00	554 6.00	500 5.50	495 6.00	426 5.50	380 4.50	358 4.30	351 4.30	371 4.40	339 4.30	370 5.00	316 4.30	246 3.20	197 3.00	213 2.40	156 2.10	108 1.30	72 1.00	80 1.20	308 4.00	255 3.30	67 1.00	52 1.00	80 1.20	129 2.00
	367 4.40	408 5.00	425 5.10	289 4.00	289 4.00	220 3.30	220 3.30	149 2.40	110 2.00	48 0.50	41 0.50	158 2.30	182 2.40	224 3.10	234 3.40	95 1.50	139 2.50	345 4.10	287 3.50	283 3.50	241 3.10	545 3.20	530 6.40	515 6.40	385 4.50	367 4.40	400 5.20	441 5.40

TORDESILHAS.
O TRATADO QUE DIVIDIU O MUNDO

Vasco Graça Moura

O TRATADO DE TORDESILHAS

THE TREATY OF TORDESILLAS

Exclusive to

CLUBE DO COLECCIONADO

CTT CORREIO
SERVIÇOS DE FILATE
Av. Casal Ribeiro, 28
1096 LISBOA CODEX

TORDESILLAS.
THE TREATY THAT DIVIDED THE WORLD

"In March 1494, the missions negotiating the treaty finally met at Tordesillas. There were high dignatories from both of the courts..."

"During the negotiations the Portuguese King seems to have put into operation an expedite service of espionage and of the buying and transmission of information, which succeeded in penetrating the most secret machinations and decisions of the councellors of Isabella and Ferdinando."

Politics, diplomacy, intrigue, alliances, compromises, marriages....
To learn more of the treaty that increased the powers of Portugal and Spain, don't miss this book containing many fascinating facts and figures from 500 years of history.

ON SALE AT THE POST OFFICE

THE TREATY OF TORDESILLAS
108 luxurious, large format pages (24.5 x 24.5 cm) · Illustrated with dozens of photographs and reproductions of maps, engravings and paintings of the period. · Illustrated with six authentic examples of stamps from Portugal, Brazil, Spain and Cape Verde commemorating 500 years of the Treaty, together with a colour proof produced, numbered and authenticated by the Mint · Text by author Vasco Graça Moura in Portuguese and English · Limited edition of 1,500 copies, numbered and authenticated by the Post Office · Volume VI of the "Discovery Collection" edited by the Post Office "Collector's Club".

Medal
e de Viseu 1992, Sogrape - Vinícola do Vale
io

Medals
a Cooperativa de Silgueiros 1991
Vasco 1992, Sogrape - Vinícola do Vale do

D'Orca 1991, Adega Coop. de V. N. Tazém
a do Pereiro 1989, Augusto Henrique de
ida C. Lopes
a do Serrado 1991, Carvalho, Ribeiro &
ra
omingos 1991, Caves do Solar de São
ngos

Commendations
ndre Magno 1990, Caves do Casalinho
ça 1992, Caves Aliança
7 1992, Carvalho, Ribeiro & Ferreira
s Velhas 1992, Caves Velhas - Comp. Port. de
os de Marca
quino 1991, A. Henriques - Caves da
anha
a da Espinhosa 1991, Alberto de Oliveira

a da Ribeira 1990, Augusto Henrique de
ida C. Lopes
a dos Roques 1991, Quinta dos Roques -
nicultura e Agro-Pecuária
a dos Roques 1992, Quinta dos Roques -
nicultura e Agro-Pecuária
to 1991, Udaca - União das Adegas Coop. do

WINES

Medals
ça Garrafeira 1984, Caves Aliança
olibri 1980, Empresa Vinícola Vilanovense
erras Altas 1986, José Maria da Fonseca
e de Viseu 1990, Sogrape - Vinícola do Vale
io
Vasco 1990, Sogrape - Vinícola do Vale do

Vasco Garrafeira 1985, Sogrape - Vinícola do
lo Dão
Mundo 1985, Caves Acácio - Vinhos de
gal
a da Espinhosa 1970, Alberto de Oliveira

a da Espinhosa 1980, Alberto de Oliveira

a das Maias 1990, Soc. Agr. Faldas da Serra
a dos Roques 1990, Quinta dos Roques -
nicultura e Agro-Pecuária
a dos Roques 1991, Quinta dos Roques -
nicultura e Agro-Pecuária
to 1989, Udaca - União das Adegas Coop. do

Medals
a Coop. Silgueiros 1990
ndre Magno 1988, Caves do Casalinho
ça Reserva 1989, Caves Aliança
cão 1990, Caves do Barrocão
7 1989, Carvalho, Ribeiro & Ferreira
da Ínsua 1988, José Maria da Fonseca
anho 1988, Caves do Casalinho
a Martins 1985, União Comercial da Beira
aves Velhas 1989, Caves Velhas - Comp.
de Vinhos de Marca
eserva 1985, Caves Dom Teodósio
D. Henrique 1990, Adega Coop. de
ualde
D. Henrique Reserva 1989, Adega Coop. de
ualde
as 1980, Soc. Agr. e Comercial dos Vinhos
as
as 1985, Soc. Agr. e Comercial dos Vinhos
as
as Dão 1990, Soc. Agr. e Comercial dos
s Messias
stico 1985, União Comercial da Beira
D'Orca 1987, Adega Coop. de V. N. Tazém
D'Orca 1989, Adega Coop. de V. N. Tazém
a da Espinhosa 1979, Alberto de Oliveira

a da Espinhosa 1985, Alberto de Oliveira

a das Maias Especial 1990, Soc. Agr. Faldas
ra
a do Serrado 1990, Carvalho, Ribeiro &
ra
aio 1990, Adega Coop. de S. Paio
omingos 1987, Caves do Solar de São
ngos
omingos 1989, Caves do Solar de São
agos
omingos 1990, Caves do Solar de São
ngos
to 1987, Udaca - União das Adegas Coop. do

Garrafeira 1980, Udaca - União das Adegas
do Dão

Commendations
cão Reserva 1989, Caves do Barrocão
olibri 1983, Empresa Vinícola Vilanovense
a da Espinhosa 1984, Alberto de Oliveira

a do Pereiro 1989, Augusto Henrique de
ida C. Lopes

The youthful spirit of a venerable region

Today's DÃO wines are an alliance of age-old tradition and modern technology.

Noble grape varieties have been nutured to perfection. Ancestral knowledge has been fused with sophisticated technical developments in viticultural methods. A careful synthesis of science and nature's bounty has produced unique wines of distinction and remarkable character.

It is not surprising, therefore, that DÃO wines have been honoured with the greatest number of awards in Portugal's 8th Concurso Nacional de Vinhos Engarrafados . They received no less than 62 gold and silver medals and high commendations in this prestigious national competition.

This is yet another important recognition of the youthful spirit that pervades a venerable region.

Comissão Vitivinícola Regional do Dão
Federação dos Vinicultores do Dão

*Choose
·
your
·
Regional
·
Restaurant
·
from our
·
menu
·*

 RESTAURANTS
POUSADAS DE PORTUGAL

GENERAL INFORMATION

T **ravel documents** - Passports are necessary for all foreign visitors. Visas are not needed by EC nationals, Americans, Canadians, Australians or New Zealanders.

Language - English and to a lesser extent French and German are spoken by many of the Portuguese people with whom foreign visitors commonly come into contact in pousadas, restaurants, banks, shops and places of recreation. Language is seldom a problem although the majority of Portugese speak only their mother tongue. Even in very remote areas it is not uncommon to find a German or French-speaking villager, probably on holiday or retired from employment overseas.

Pousada reservations - These may be made through ENATUR, Av. Santa Joana Princesa 10 A, 1700 Lisbon; telephone 01-8481221/8489078/8484602 ; telex 13609/63475/64243 ENATUR P; fax 01- 805846/8484349. We advise making your reservation by fax or telex. Bookings may also be made by contacting individual pousadas directly. If possible, bookings should be made well in advance.

Payment - Accommodation and all services at pousadas may be paid for in cash, by travellers' cheques or by credit card.

Driving - Drive on the right. The speed limits are 60 kph (33 mph) in built-up zones, 90 kph (56 mph) on the open road and 120 kph (75 mph) on motorways. If stopped by traffic police, drivers must be able to show a valid licence, vehicle registration, insurance document, and a letter of authorisation if the vehicle is owned by other than the occupants. If you are hiring a car make sure all likely drivers

are covered in the contract. In the event of an accident involving another vehicle, exchange names and adresses and insurance details. If there is serious damage or injury, the police must be informed as soon as possible. Petrol stations are scarce out of the main towns and off the main highways, so keep a careful eye on your fuel guage.

Money - The unit of currency is the escudo variously written as Esc. 1, one escudo or 1$00. The numbers after the $ sign refer to centavos, now virtually worthless. The coin denominations are 1$00 (hardly used), 2$50, 5$00, 10$00, 20$00, 50$00, 100$00 and 200$00. The notes are for 500, 1,000, 2,000, 5,000 and 10,000 escudos.

Banks - Exchange facilities are available at airports for all arriving and departing flights. Some, though not all, frontier posts have exchange facilities. Normal banks offering all the usual services open 8.30 am to 3 pm Monday to Friday; closed on weekends and public holidays. Our advice would be to obtain a nominal amount of escudos before leaving home to avoid unnecessary delay on arrival.

Postal Services - Hours vary, but most of the larger post offices open from 8.30 am to 6 pm Monday to Friday. The smaller ones close for lunch. Services include international telephone and, in some cases, fax facilities.

Tourist offices - a great many towns frequented by visitors have a signposted *Turismo* office where English, French and German-speaking receptionists should be able to supply literature and help you with most queries. The headquarters of the National Tourist Office is at Av. António Augusto de Aguiar 86, 1000 Lisbon; telephone 01 575086; fax 01 556917. There are Portuguese National Tourism Offices in London, Frankfurt and throughout the world.

Electricity - The voltage is 220 AC. Applicances need two-pin plugs or adapters.

Tipping - Pousadas and most restaurants include all taxes and service charges in their bills, but in appreciation for good service a tip is in order for porters, maids and waiters. Waiters greatly appreciate a tip of 5 to 10% in addition to the service charge.

Shopping - Shops commonly close for lunch between 1 pm and 3 pm weekdays, on Saturday afternoon, all day Sunday and public holidays. Fixed prices are the norm. A certain amount of haggling goes on for such things as clothes, leather goods and other products in regional markets.

An ideal gift: Algarve almond cakes. MK

Public Holidays - The main public holidays are January 1, April 25, Good Friday, May 1, Corpus Christi in June or July, June 10, August 15, October 5, November 1, December 1, December 8 and December 25. There are other local public holidays which may close offices, banks, shops, museums and monuments for the day.

Emergencies - Dial 115 anywhere in Portugal for police, fire or ambulance. Pousada reception desks and tourist information offices among other places have lists of doctors, dentists and consulates. Consulates are located in Lisbon, Oporto and Algarve. Pharmacies keep normal shop hours, but each town always has one open at night on a rota basis for prescriptions.

TOWN INDEX

Alijó, Pousada Barão de Forrester, **46**
Alcácer do Sal, Vale do Gaio, **124**
Almeida, Senhora das Neves, **54**
Alvito, Castelo, **164**
Amarante, São Gonçalo, **50**
Aveiro, da Ria, **58**
Batalha, Mestre A. Domingues, **78**
Beja, Convento de S. Francisco, **170**
Bragança, São Bartolomeu, **38**
Caniçada, São Bento, **22**
Caramulo, São Jerónimo, **66**
Condeixa-a-Nova, Santa Cristina, **150**
Crato, Mosteiro de Flor da Rosa, **170**
Elvas, Santa Luzia, **114**
Estremoz, Rainha Santa Isabel, **108**
Évora, dos Lóios, **118**
Guimarães, Nossa Senhora de Oliveira, **28**
        - Santa Marinha da Costa, **32**
Lisbon, Palácio de Queluz, **171**
Manteigas, São Lourenço, **74**
Marvão, Santa Maria, **104**
Miranda do Douro, Santa Catarina, **42**
Monsanto, de Monsanto, **158**
Óbidos, Do Castelo, **82**
Oliveira do Hospital, Santa Bárbara, **70**
Palmela, de Palmela, **88**
Sagres, Do Infante, **144**
Santa Clara-a-Velha, Santa Clara, **136**
Santiago do Cacém, São Tiago, **128**
            - Quinta da Ortiga, **148**
São Brás de Alportel, São Brás, **140**
Serém, Santo António, **62**
Serpa, São Gens, **132**
Setúbal, São Filipe, **94**
Sousel, São Miguel, **154**
Tomar, São Pedro, **100**
Valença do Minho, São Teotónio, **14**
Vila Nova de Cerveira, Dom Dinis, **18**